# THE
# CAGE
# CLEANERS
# OF
# JERUSALEM

# THE CAGE CLEANERS OF JERUSALEM

EMELY BATIN-ORILLOS

authorHOUSE®

*AuthorHouse™*
*1663 Liberty Drive*
*Bloomington, IN 47403*
*www.authorhouse.com*
*Phone: 1 (800) 839-8640*

*Published by AuthorHouse 09/03/2019*

*ISBN: 978-1-7283-2560-6 (sc)*
*ISBN: 978-1-7283-2581-1 (hc)*
*ISBN: 978-1-7283-2559-0 (e)*

*Library of Congress Control Number: 2019912976*

*Print information available on the last page.*

to my late husband, LORENZO Q. ORILLOS
"O Jerusalem, Jerusalem
how often
would have I gathered
thy children together
even as a hen
gathered her chickens
under her wings…"

[Matthew 23: 37]

# Contents

# *Preface*

THIS STORY IS WRITTEN TO chronicle a life once lived...lives in the seasons of grace. Mine is told for me to live again...to forgive the sunset for its deception, to remember the gentle rain for the hope it brings to the child's heart, to pray with the coming of a new day...to bask in the grace of penitence ...ultimately, to be grateful for the "miracle" of JERUSALEM.

A Place. The Star. Bethlehem. The Holy Manger. The Good Shepherds. The Three Noble Kings. Joy. Love. Salvation. JERUSALEM.

This book is not just mine. Actually, it has never been mine. It belongs to Him who makes all things right, to Him who came in all humility. And He wants me to share with each and everyone the Gift of the Manger... one life of a child who used to copy the BOOK OF LIFE while she also played in the radiance of the gracious sun. Yes, simple as it is, as it can be. But JERUSALEM is eternity. This life is more than blessed though the weight of the CROSS almost crushed it to waste in desolation. At least not now. And never will be. JERUSALEM keeps its promise. This book is a gift of that child...with her home nestled in the "manger" nearby THE HOLY ONE...a dream or legend, it is a tale to tell. So a PROEM to that story now follows:

**Our hands were always full since they came. We really did not mind. They led us to a "manger."**

**To JERUSALEM. We are THE CAGE CLEANERS, and this is our story.**

**EBO 2019**

ix

"O GOD, YOU ARE MY GOD WHOM I SEEK; FOR YOU MY
FLESH PINES AND MY SOUL THIRSTS LIKE THE EARTH,
PARCHED, LIFELESS AND WITHOUT WATER."

(Psalm 63:2)

*Chapter One*

---

# The Great March

THEY ARE NOT AS MANY. I had the big one cut down last summer. While it had plenty of those succulent greens and the branches, the vines held so many secrets, memories, oh yes, memories, it needed trimming. Had I followed my heart, I would have just whispered my wish every now and then but everyone said the chainsaw was badly needed. Besides I feared the heavy rains. The longer, heavier boughs might fall on the Grotto of Our Lady...on the silent tomb...the black granite with maroon edges...where the man who used to feed daily for almost a decade some thirty or more wild but yet domesticated feline and a sweet gentle loving canine, now lies in eternal repose...under the Mango trees of my childhood...surrounded by them like the loyal sentinels of the British Monarch, the Gurkha of the great Himalayas...watching over his grave with the prayerful hands and loving face of the Blessed Mother, while fruits abound each day yet fall into the much less glossy top of the cold sanctuary, mornings and evenings, whether one hot summer day or just another night of dolor and forlorn. This man was Enzo, my husband. The old Indian Mango tree by the eastern side of our fading purple gate used to be full of Christmas lights, well, like the one on the left west, its trunk leaning so warmly on the

1

ground; it glittered with the diamonds of a joyful home under December skies. Yes, especially when our precious moments in the earliest wellsprings of great true love were just beginning to bask in the blissful grace of God's greatest gift to mankind. The loving husband. The trees of love.

Today is 22 October 2018.

I have just cleaned the mess[oh, diamonds!]of our twelve year-old Labrador, with a long but most beautiful and sentimental name--- Mary Nazarene Paula Erlinda Cassiopeia. We fondly call her "Linda," abbreviated name of my late dearest older sister, ERLEEN, whom we'd call "ERLINDA!," with the perfect big brown hazel eyes, in jest or in scorn among siblings of eight, all names beginning in letter "E"[Eloida, Elrey, Erleen, Millie, Ely, Estela Marie, Errol Anthony, Ethel Consuelo]. The two younger ones are our siblings from our father's second nuptial. Oh, our dog's history traces its legend or miracle[?] with one of Jesus's favoured, Saul of Tarsus. Yes, she came from the home of those pious, religious, and devoted women with the great saint as their patron, the Sisters of St. Paul[SPC]of Chartres. Mary Nazarene Paula Erlinda Cassiopeia bears the magic or the grace of that LIGHT that signalled the birth of a SAVIOUR. She is of the same age as JP, our only child. My now orphan son since 2017.

While Earth was plagued by the havoc of a sudden storm on the night of 9 August 2010, a gentle-faced cat of graceful movement walked like a queen into our *sala* as if nature's fury was just another song that missed its lyrics or went out of tune. It was the eve of my husband's 62nd birthday. JP was three years old, and that night, our little child opened our old door for the BEGINNING of our sojourn, a one of a kind peregrination, yes, a marvellous grand *paseo…*

A PILGRIMAGE of an ordinary simple family to the "manger" of JERUSALEM…

As she moved in confident careful gait to a corner, her eyes met mine. They were bluish and black green. They were calm and warm. My heart felt them, and she made a soft purr as she cuddled in her brown, black, and white mystical being. Oh, I was ecstatic in spirit yet I had no words to utter that moment. JP then sat beside the gentle thing, caressing her body with his little and tender hands while his pyjamas seemed to cackle in indescribable joy with the unexpected coming of a visitor. A VERY SPECIAL AND REGAL QUEEN. She was then named KITTY, HER ROYAL HIGHNESS. The downpour was nonetheless unimpressed yet its onslaught eventually came to an end; that's nature in its natural cycle. But Kitty? She stayed for nine years. And she never meant to be alone. She came with a noble and loyal throng, her royal court. One after the other. Until Enzo, Millie, and JP were now to find themselves in a "manger" in that Holy Land. Of a dog, and dozens of feline. Hence, the small ordinary family of three became the home of THE CAGE CLEANERS OF JERUSALEM since that stormy night of 9 August 2010. But before Kitty came with her royal court, some seven or eight unusually big wild cats who looked like the council of elders walked past our suburban home, around three o'clock in the morning one time I was hanging the laundry by our garage. It was odd that they were all looking at me from the street, and seemed to be talking also about me! I felt something special was to happen though I got the goose bumps all over! Then, her Royal Highness stood by our door while it rained so hard that night of August, with the rest of her loyal throng to follow on a dramatic march! From then on, our home life took on a very extraordinary twist, with our extended family of a variety of feline and our Labrador! Tale of old or the legend of a lowly pen, the story continues for the faith is overflowing with grace, inspired by a Supreme Being whose perfect ways are always tales of mystery, told and re-told over thousands and thousands of years. This is just perhaps one side story of the zillions. But what makes it a little more is IT DID HAPPEN. My heart knows it fully well…now. And still, it continues to tell its tale. Allegory or epical, it does not really matter. What is of virtue is its perfection or of its struggle for perfection of its JERUSALEM.

Linda would just gently bark on each one as they marched like dukes and duchesses into our undeserving home of cheap paintings but of beautiful colors and honest strokes, of leaking roofs yet of the legacy of Filipino erudition. Our humble home was situated at a dead end, with a most legendary Acacia tree right there in our backyard, and a big funeral home that has a crematorium[Oh, we just got used to that "odd smell" through the years!] just beside our falling fence though graced by nontoxic mushrooms and prolific kamias[Averrhoa bilimbi] that street children would beg to pick right where they sprouted so enviously profuse and inviting. Undergraduate Mass Communication students would also keep calling by our gate if they could do a film shoot in our home as it had the look of either a peaceful or haunted house.

They indeed came strong, each with a legend, each one with a tale, aside from their cute wonderful tails. The GRACE of JERUSALEM was astoundingly magical, blissful but not without the difficulties, dangers, and threats of that HOLY NIGHT IN THE MANGER. The years that followed saw the cage cleaners work dutifully with their hands, at times in glee, in most times, in tears of sorrow and remorse yet those tears would always bind the family with Jesus and the Holy Family as their source of strength and inspiration. Here's a roll call to that noble line that took a simple family of a doting husband, a somewhat "odd" wife, and a well-loved child to an unlikely unbelievable yet truthfully amazing sojourn where they found themselves no less than in a "manger" beside THE MANGER. The list may not be as accurate for the memory is still besieged by its most cruel episodes though giving its best to beat the pangs of despair, and well, the tyranny of anger including the poison of old, VENGEANCE. Of course, this is but the poesy of my wrath, the pasquinade of my pain and its indignation against medical malpractice. The list comes indeed, with the golden and darkest hours of the family's journey to Jerusalem. Here it proudly proclaims in careful chronology, the best possible listing:

1. Kitty 2. RT 3. Peter 4. Beauty 5. Garfield or Mokmok 6. Snowy 7. Gabby 8. Lucky 9. Sheila 10. Amanda 11. Amanda's twin 12. Pinky 13. Marsha 14. Amby 15. Gabby the Second 16. Gabby the Third 17. Peter the Second 18. Blacky 19. Hillary 20. Eva 21. November 22. Golgol 23. Snowbell 24. Clinton 25. Tomasa or tommy 26. Three kittens and more 27. August 28. Johny 29. Brownie 30. Enzo 31. Goring 32. Genie 33. King 34. February 35. March.

Linda now sleeps soundly on all fours. It's past one in the morning. I have to check on JP if he has signed out the laptop. He should be in bed as he has classes in Starland by twelve noon. I must be a good mother to my eleven year old. I can't afford to be negligent of his needs. He's growing much faster than my patience for my widowhood of almost two years. Yes, my child will soon be a man except that he is yet to be circumcised. I'm so scared of doctors and hospitals, with what fate came to my husband. But as I scour the Holy Bible if circumcision is a must for Christian boys, I get tossed in the depths of my guilt as both the Old and the New Testaments have parabolic accounts of the grace that comes with circumcision besides the fact that my son's former school superior would always ask me," *Natuli na ba iyan?*" everytime we bump into her in the blue planet, with my son blushing and hiding behind my schizophrenia and paranoia. Oh, my coffee is cold. As usual. Hmm, the chicken *adobo* makes my stomach crave for the old plate. I wonder if those tomatoes in the vegetable crisper are still crisp and fresh, but oh, I've got a nice bottle of the best Ilocos *boggoong* [fish sauce]. Do I really want to eat or should I just kiss the Holy Feet? If only there was no memory. But they come like the gust of an early breeze, and my soul quivers. Oh God, the chicken *adobo* flares up like ranting stars in my tiny rice cooker turned frying pan! Indeed, I should not forget. Anyway, I no longer sleep at night. The sun will be out again soon. Another day. Kitty, with her light blue necklace[very special, given by the earth fairy], purrs softly and looks at me with her gentle eyes before she goes to slumber party. What loving eyes that send tears once more to my heart…

Tonight is 19 May 2019.

I just buried Kitty. We just did as the sun was high. Not that I was really fully attentive of the quiet ceremony for my subconscious just preferred to let the moment drift away, unnoticed, to buffer the pain. I carried her carefully in that light green box to finally lay her to rest beside the tomb of her good Master, my husband. Somehow, it felt better. Yes, it does. After the summer class, JP and I had to hurry home from our rabbit's hole in the Metropolis to bury our QUEEN in this spot, under the Indian Mango trees, by the Blessed Mother's Grotto. We kept her well-wrapped in her light green box for more than two weeks, and it was unbelievable that there wasn't any of that terrible smell, even as we travelled for almost thirteen hours! When she breathed her last five minutes before midnight of April 30, 2019, I just couldn't stop from my heavy sobs that JP was so worried and scared I might have a heart attack for my blood pressure has become unstable since 2017, and I've not been seeing any single doctor or cardiologist! Hence, I don't really have what should be "safe" medicine except for my guts and well, silliness. My most legendary most special cat looked at me so lovingly, purred softly, extended her left front foot to reach my fingers, then she died. Her Royal Highness said her good-bye in such a heartrending, heart- breaking way that I wept until the wee hours while JP silently wiped his tears with the palm of his hands. Then, the metaphysical rhapsody of the first dawn of May; my experimental genre, *ANG PAG-UUSAP NG PALAKA AT MATSING:Metapisika Ng Buwan* or... [Quiambao 2019, in the works]. Kitty made her last and SUPREME SACRIFICE. Had I not wept until dawn, the dew drops would not have pried into the subrosa of the tallest red rose in Eden, not so much of Wilde's "The Rose And The Nightingale"[!], and hence, such perfect mystery my lowly pen might not have unravelled in the very complication of life's metafiction, which takes the form of my humble second modest novel in the making--- DOUBLECROSS OF THE PINK PANTHER, OH, COUGAR! [Quiambao 2019, in the works]. Yes, my cat's legend will forever live in my heart! My brother-in-law, Guillermo "Guiller" Abarquez was drenched in sweat and perspiration late that afternoon [yesterday, 18 May 2019], as he dug patiently the destined hole, the rightful resting place for the ROYAL QUEEN OF MY MENAGERIE, now as I call it. Our little zoo has greatly waned in size. I'm not sure if their magic or miracle continues from today. Especially now that Kitty, all wrapped up in my favorite white embroidered blanket is lying there in her mint green box, not exactly six feet under the ground but beside her great decent loving Master. Yes, Kitty rests now with my beloved under the Indian Mangoes, by the Yellow Bells, and by the magical Dorantha, a desert plant with fragile lovely purple flowers, like the spring or Easter Pasqueflower [and so, the Holy Feet love the purple cologne especially at midnight!]. I laid my Aunt Fely's bounteous African bougainvillea all over my legendary cat's final resting nook. A tear fell on that mound of familiar earth, surrounded by little and big stones of my ancestry. I knew I'd be missing my Royal Highness forever...[My tribute in a song of prayer, "Her Royal Highness" is in the Appendices!]

We were in Jerusalem. All three of us---husband, wife, child. Plus our dog and cats. For almost nine years...

This dawn makes me sigh more as I recall how wonderful it was that life we had as cage cleaners. My spirit refuses to crush though for every mistake, every terrible sin I could have avoided while my home was in Jerusalem. It could have been BETHLEHEM, JERUSALEM. But it was close…

O JERUSALEM, O JERUSALEM!
Such tranquillity and peace!
Perfect joy, O Serenity in the Twilight…While doom impels the babies' cries! Upon your Bosom, Eternity rejoices; the harp and lyre create Sanctuaries for the soul. None shines as bright as the Radiance of the Star which reigned o'er fear and terror; The Manger bore the Saviour! Alas, the world was deep in slumber, just the Magi and the shepherds, for the Cage Cleaners had their hands full, they didn't see The Miracle though they felt the glow and heard the baby's mirthful coos as their pets rejoiced!

[EBO 2019]

# Chapter Two

## "Lilies of the Fields" and the Tree Climber: One Little Indian War Girl

"MILLIE, *APO KO, ANIA DAYTA ar-aramidem*?" [What preoccupies my grandchild?]

My granny, *Lilang* Alejandra "Andang" Tejada-Pimentel smiles with her Virginia *tabako* [tobacco], puffing freely in the air a life of joy and sacrifice. Since our mother, *Mamang Lourdes,* with Castilian descent, succumbed to brain tumor at age thirty-seven, our granny has never left us longer than a week. Just once. When she and her younger sister, *Auntie* Nellie, a public school English and Science teacher, went to the Western Visayas Region of the Philippines, Iloilo to visit our grandpa, *Lolo* Celine who sat then in a university as its President. Our grandfather was more than lucky to study at the University of Missouri in the United States of America for his Ph.D. in Education so was our *Lolo* Modesto, who specialized in Zoology for his doctorate in that same U.S. university; both with scholarships. Our granny was second to a brood of nine. All her siblings, except the eldest [who was killed in WWII], got good education, with *Lolo* Alfredo "Pedong" a lawyer then an RTC Judge of Mamburao, Mindoro; *Lolo* Dinong, a Principal of Caloocan Public School; *Lolo* Juaning a Professor in a state university in Vigan, *Auntie* Mayyang, a business woman in Occidental, Mindoro; of course aside from American-schooled *Lolo* Celine and *Lolo* Modesto, and *Auntie* Nellie, a graduate of then Philippine Normal College or PNC whom we dearly called as such for her closeness to us while growing up, and considering her much younger age than our *Lilang* Andang. Typical of an Ilocana eldest daughter, our granny forgot her own dreams to help our great grandparents, *Lolo* Baak and *Lola* Enriqueta send her younger siblings to school, thus, she finished only up to Grade Three [but with incredible good conversational English!]. Such a selfless woman who had the most beautiful of dutiful hands and loving eyes! *Lilang* Andang was a gentle and caring soul whose faith was resplendent of all splendored things! Early in the morning and at dusk, our granny would be praying, reciting the Holy Rosary in our mother tongue, Ilocano, complete with her beautiful veils of delicate lace that I'd always loved to touch as a child! I was so much a tactile eager learner, quite fascinated with the mystery of veils aside from my proclivity for singing skies, waters, and earth, and star gazing at night! On Sundays, granny would get up so early to go to St. Catherine Church at the *parada* or town proper of Santa, Ilocos Sur. This historic church sits metaphorically beautiful in a little square facing a great sea as that of Jerusalem's Bethlehem! Our *Lilang* would teach us all the prayers and how to kneel before *Apo Lakay* [Santo Kristo]. She was the perfect grandmother of six orphans. *Mamang* Lourdes was her only child to that handsome foreman- postman, Filipino-Hispanic *Lolo* Rafael "Paeng" Pimentel [from Sta. Lucia], who, unfortunately, while carrying all those precious letters and trekking the Cordilleras, was shot by the enemy during the war, our *Lolo* serving then the Filipino soldiers as their secret courier. But *Lilang* Andang had both good and horrible stories to tell us of that historic period in the country. Especially during bedtime, and when the stars were hanging a-plenty in Ilocos skies. When our *Papang* [father], Teofilo "Eloy" Batin was out of town for his job with the Department of Agriculture as its Region 1 Director, checking on all the produce and seeds of the good soil, concocting with his colleagues MASAGANA 99 to assure the country with the best rice and corn. Oh, granny had all of the best stories, tales, fables, and legends of the universe to tell us, including riddles while we were all but young, playful, and tender. She loved all six of us but the fourth child would usually make her smile, laugh more, and verse her own wonderful maxims, oh words of wit and wisdom while she'd puff her Virginia *tabako*, multi-tasking [doing the laundry with her able indefatigable hands, ironing our clothes, our boy scout and girl scout uniforms with the flat iron like a steaming speeding train along dangerous ravines and over deep rivers. Oh, *Lilang would be* cooking and boiling all kinds of beans and heavenly stew, brewing every possible herb that sprouted in our yard and the open fields behind our bungalow that sat on a cliff of old so covered later by willing earth, dishing out every exotic meal of tasteful farm frogs in rich orange sauce, flavoured by the *kamias,* and fleshy *igat* [eel] with the aroma of the mystic underworld, delighting our lazy afternoons with every delectable native delicacy of *suman*[rice cakes], *biko, bibingka, puto, palitaw, binuelos, budol, guinatan, banana and camote cues,* etc., following up on the women blanket-weavers of the famous Ilocos *ules,* counting the colourful heavy comfort, then selling them whole sale or retail, going door-to-door in all possible corners of the planet with their frivolous weight on her good head, her long hair pulled tightly and nicely to a bun, and dozens more on both her diligent beautiful hands, those Ilocos pride tied too neatly and securely for the hardworking uncomplaining Ilocana to barter with the gracious and welcoming families that longed for more warmth and sound sleep during the wet season or the rainy days. *Lilang* would then come home with all the good harvests, sweets, and dried fish, with her six grandchildren jumping in and out of joy while the other bus commuters and passers by would smile and watch in glee and warm affectionate admiration for the kind-hearted hardworking granny and the sweet innocent orphans as the life size and half busts of the elegant Spanish Senora, a former Miss College of Education of Far Eastern University [FEU], Manila in her heydays glistened in the sun with her rose garden and purple orchids, filling the cool air with all those heavenly fragrance and scent of pristine freshness and nature's best.

I let my granny take a good look at my child's play. Around this time, I'm still beginning to learn to read much faster on my own and to write with better strokes the letters of the English Alphabet. Maybe, the girl with short hair and cute bangs [a la Beetles!] is eight or nine. Her bond papers are lying full in merriment on the sparkling tiles of their love-filled *sala* as the art, culture, and music of that elegant so fair woman of a natural blonde and curls grace every wall, every table, every window of their bungalow painted in the colors of the sun, the open fields, the fire trees, and the romance of roses and wild orchids.

"Oh, my grandchild, you are copying The Book!" *Lilang* Andang is obviously delighted and perplexed. She gently touches my shoulder as she proceeds with her chores in the kitchen where sunlight never misses to dance on every glorious day. Black beans and pork spare ribs topped with the fine greens of Ilocandia and flavoured by the region' famous fish sauce with all those young onions and best garlic are waiting for her final secret ingredients of devoted love and unwavering piety plus a bottle of the *takong's* [mother pig] *manteka* [oil], her incomparable stew for her grandchildren of five girls and one boy to savor, each in their delicate Chinese porcelain bowls for lunch and then supper, with the full moon and the stars to grace the usual evenings of six orphans and a noble selfless woman who keeps a *lakasa, a baul* [treasure chest!] of the magical secrets of life. How the little ones would snuggle by their grandmother's warm body as she'd tell them after supper of how the sudden invasion of the enemy in the 1940's, their formidable arrival at Santa shores by the China Sea, one night of stillness and quietude, turned upside down their peaceful and simple existence, unsuspecting of the danger that came in a fleet, riding on top of giant waves in the grayness of a starless night. Oh, *Lilang* Andang had tears in her eyes as she'd recount of the horrors of that night where the townsfolk scampered like rats and roaches [quite a biting thematic contrast to Bienvenido Lumbera's "Eulogy of Roaches"] in every hole and crevice in the dark, with many running, fleeing to the mountains, leaving their hard earned little treasures and happy memories behind except that her own family in Banaoang chose to hide under their beds and under the wooden staircase with three year-old Lourdes wondering why they were all up so late at night and the old folks mumbling strange words while praying the rosary in between their prattle and rattle and scamper. Ah, *Lolo* Juaning, granny's much younger brother had his own tales of the war. In fact, his tales were even more horrible for he'd act them out as he recounted the episodes in all the prosody and segmentals of the holocaust like when he and his brother [*Lolo* Pedong] escaped the historic Death March, with their feet and hands in chains! "Oh, we ran, galloped, and ran like hell and hid in the bushes so the enemies won't see us! *Lolo* Juaning would pant and gasp for air as he'd tumble and run to and fro our front door before our big, wide opened eyes and mouths, our small bodies trembling in fear and fright, for our grandpa's voice thundered like a crushing helicopter by the mountains of our dreams and youthful adventures, seemingly not sparing a single black or red wild berry that filled our tiny bellies whenever they complained. Oh, those luscious sweet berries were abundant by the foot of Sleeping Beauty, the legendary mountain of Santa, Ilocos Sur, with its magical greatness kissing the bashful but grateful clouds. *Lolo* Juaning would visit us as often as *Auntie* Nellie, with him repeating every now and then his grand escape with his younger brother, *Lolo* Pedong, and of course, his truly frightening acts, complete with a plastic of fresh *bunog* and *sisiaw* [fresh fish], sending those sweet prudent smiles on the gentle lovely face of *Lilang* Andang early mornings and even before dusk. She'd likewise hand her younger sibling a dozen of sweet *chikoo* or nispero, and *chesa* or canistel, from our orchard of such fantastic fruit-bearing trees we'd climb like the happiest baby monkeys that were literally plenty during those times, our house situated close to the mountain ranges of Ilocos Sur. But then, *Lilang* would also remind her *Ading* [younger brother] how the good Japanese soldiers of WWII loved *Mamang* Lourdes [reminding them of their own children back home!] as they'd play with her and give her candies for she was such an adorable three year-old with long curly tresses. *Lolo* Juaning would come driving in his handsome motorbike, wearing casual shirts, walking shorts, comfy footwear, and a cool hat with Marlboro in his mouth. He was every inch a WWII veteran with a soft heart for his orphaned grandchildren. Much later, when our dashing knights in shining armor came in our lives, *Lolo Juaning* would hide in the basket the best fish, hung it on the kitchen ceiling as he waited for them to visit him during the *barrio* fiesta. *Auntie* Nelly, on the other hand, would teach us social skills, to be felicitous and cordial especially with the elders, and how to pronounce and enunciate in English like the schooled Filipino elite and intellectuals, the so-called *edulects* by Filipino linguists, Andrew Gonzales and Lourdes Bautista. An excellent English teacher, *Auntie* Nelly would teach the word classes [parts of speech] in context, like when she introduced nouns and verbs to us, that she used fun games and sending us shouting, running to the green board, writing the names of our neighbors and what they do every day of their lives! How the American English cadence was so richly stout, dense, and flamboyant in the tongue of our very dedicated aunt, most especially whenever she conversed over a game of cards with disciplinarian spinster, *Maestra* Senang, and her brother, our public school Principal, Mr. Jose Custodio [Australian-based *Manang* Carolyn and *Manang* Joy's dad!], a very handsome and perfectly neat man who smelled so good like the open fields of golden rice and glorious flowery shrubs and those magical herbs! All three would comment on the weather in very literary English as they'd carefully look at their cards through their thick respectable eye glasses: "*Manong*, it's good the azure skies are happy with us!" "Ah, indeed, the clouds aren't a bit hovering with their gloom!" "We must be fortunate as Prometheus knows our misery when the storm comes!" How my eager ears would be as large as those of my imaginary friends! Oh, *Maestro* Jose was every bit the ideal very decent school manager or dignified *pasha* that one day he invited me in his very nice office of fragrant fresh *rosal*, green and yellow floral curtains, neat piles of paper, mug of coffee, and Virginia *tabako* to let me see two new big books that have been donated by a good man to our public school which didn't really have, in those days, a library! It turned out the gracious book donor was no less than our *Papang* [father] Eloy! Oh, how proud I was of my father but I'd then fret why he gave those two history books away without my *Manang* Erleen reading them to me first! Well, our grannies and grandpas never wanted to be just simply doting grandparents too. On some occasions, another of our grandpa, *Lolo* Pedong, the strict and stern-looking Judge of Mamburao, with his rich *haciendera* mestiza wife, *Lola* Letty would pay us a visit, and he'd ask us what English words we knew over lunch of *lauya* [beef stew or pochero with the best *saba*, a variety of bananas, cabbage, potatoes, and Baguio beans!], and grilled pork liver with blushing fresh tomatoes sliced in fine thin pieces, good and easy to the bite of the now turned litigator judge to his scared *apos* [grandchildren], except that one seems more than excited to recite, impress, and spell those treasured English lexemes before an impatient judge, busy chewing the almost burned pork liver while his classy wife eats like a duchess with her large glittering jewelry of magnificent ruby, emerald, and gold, her fine dining movements catching the curious and admiring eyes of everyone but not so much the late *Lola* Petra, *Lolo* Juaning's pretty seamstress of an amusing naughty wife who'd make face behind the former governor's daughter, her sister-in-law, and sending us, kids, to giggles and chuckles before the bountiful grace. *Lolo* Dinong, a very reserved man who had the same perfect loving eyes as our granny and every inch an excellent decent principal, was more discreet but as expectant and expecting of those English words as if they were priceless foods for the gods and cherubs. Almost all of his eight children [Uncle Victor, *Auntie* Tessie, *Auntie* Lita, *Auntie* Evelyn *Auntie* Arleen, *Auntie* Rowena, Uncle Beyot, Uncle Teteng] were public school teachers, so dedicated and hardworking, who'd also give us some crash English lessons in their bright and immaculately clean, very decent uniforms whenever we'd travel to Manila in our father's comfy American style owner jeep, driven by the very cautious *Tata* Mariano, our long-time family driver, and stayed in their warm Caloocan home with *Lola* Maring's hands full but always very patient and smiling, her Tagalog so gentle, so nice and endearing to the ears. In fact their home resonated of the sweetest, bubbliest, "alive and living" Tagalog/Filipino words and idioms my very young heart loved to hear and keep plus of course, the Standard American English[SAE] syntax and phonetics! We'd then be running here and there over deep and shallow canal that smelled all the toxic of the Earth while enjoying our bottles of 7-up and mongo ice drops, oh, that I relished so much, both for the gustatory and the cosmopolitan adventure I'd proudly tell my envious cousins and classmates back home. Surely, my playmates eagerly listened to my anecdotes while we played Chinese garter, *tumbang preso,* and jackstone! My voice and my pitch would be so high and low as I'd tell them of how our jeep went under those overpasses that seemed to be mouths of friendly giants, how we managed into those tortuous roads and sharp curves more like large and small intestines of some exciting creature, and the many fun times of stop overs, with our mother buying little and big pots of plants as if the gardens and vegetation at home were never enough! Or when it was Baguio, the City of Pines as another itinerary for the big family, all happily cramped up in our super jeep, *Mamang* [mother] Lourdes would bring home all those gigantic fantastic lovely roses plus ingenious wooden sculpture of a smoking elderly *Igorot* or half- naked exotic and beautiful *Igorota* [as in early history of the native women of Ifugao were ingenuously depicted, in photography, books, movies, and the arts though Resil Mojares wrote a critique of such art titled," Photography As Rape."]. Well, I'd also tell my playmates of what our granny from

Mamburao would bring and teach us whenever she visited. *Lola* Mayyang, youngest of *Lilang's* siblings, was always so sweet together with handsome, *Lolo* Ador, her adorable hubby, bringing us all those huge and delicious oysters from as far as Mindoro but they were likewise both excited to find out who was smart or smarter among the six of us, who could say apple in the American twang while they carried so carefully in their protective loving hands their adopted delicate and sickly baby girl, that spinster and single-blessed-happy-worry free, *Auntie* Nellie [but not so much in her old age, when her body and heart became weak and frail!] would discuss with our *Lilang* the seemingly sorry fate of the couple over cups of hot black coffee, meringue [whatever was left of their *pasalubong from* their Iloilo tryst, gee, that fabulous wooden boat, the Spanish galleon of the great Portuguese explorer, Ferdinand Magellan killed by the brave local hero, Lapu Lapu in Mactan! It took my breath away and made me stuff in my mouth the meringue in no time!] and banana cues in late lazy rainy afternoons. American-schooled *Lolo* Celine and *Lolo* Modesto sounded so different yet so good, so exorbitantly sophisticated, so expensive, so perfect especially to my eager little ears with strange inner contours as confirmed and diagnosed by an ear specialist in the city of now hellish traffic. Ah, our grannies and grandpas, with their indisputable great penchant for SAE, were all their own unique and interesting characters but each was never without some odd or amusing stories to tell before, during, and after meals, whether in our home or in their old but beautiful family house of wood and *capis* that strategically sat [and still is!] by the curve of the national highway; behind it, the poetic Banaoang/Abra River, on the east, the majestic Ilocos Mountain Ranges, on the northern side, the historic Quirino Bridge, named after the Ilocano Philippine President, Elpidio. *Lolo* Juaning and *Lolo* Pedong would tell us how sturdy that bridge was for it served as a Japanese garrison during the war. But wait, our own father and mother had their amazing tales too to tell especially of their love story that began in grade school[!] but after their almost nightly gala shows of dance, like Russian Waltz, jazz, cha cha, tango, boogie, the local dances, etc.! Oh, our parents were most graceful dancers! Step to the left, step to the right, forward here, forward there, a little turn, a hip to sway-God, how they'd beat Travolta and Madonna! And songs, classic and folk, modern and romance. *Papang* Eloy even wrote a number of poems and zarzuelas for our village or for his bureau that one time, the lead performers eloped after their dramatic amorous play! Oh, how the people and his employees loved him as they would come to our house early in the morning with their *bilaos* of *kamoteng kahoy* [cassava], *tugi* [Asiatic yam], fresh tomatoes, *utong* [stringbeans], giant cauliflowers, and even the delicious but precious *malaga* [tasteful fish], shrimps, crabs, and prawns grown from their own fish pens, or the rare divine tiny fish, *ipon*! Oh, before the declaration of Martial Law in 1972 by strongman, *Apo* Marcos, some strange men would knock late at night to ask for rice and food, and while they'd be sipping their hot black coffee, I and my siblings would be like peeping Toms from our underground full of dried yellow corn! *Mamang* Lourdes would likewise organize the village ladies for the fiesta cultural shows with pretty *Manang* Nessie and long-haired vixen, *Manang* Ely as the star dancers, her favorites of the Barangay Rizal damsels, of course aside from *Nana* Esteling and *Nana* Erling whom she'd gift with her very special plants, claiming their seeds came from England! Our father went to Cambridge University for special studies in Agronomy with a British-Australian Columbo Plan Scholarship. According to our *Mamang*, our father chose to bring home seeds rather than sweets from that great land! So, when I didn't get the First Place in Grade One, our pretty mestiza mother stormed to our public school, and lashed out in her Castilian idioms on my *Maestra*, accusing her of vengeance for not having been the fortunate beneficiary or recipient of her special plants from Great Britain! So I realized then why the Holy Bible starts its dozens of stories in a garden! From then on, I'd be missing in my Grade School classes, picking wild flowers, and hunting for rare weeds and shrubs! And I'd be bribing my sister Erleen with these lovely blossoms and plants for her to read aloud for me the print world! *Mamang* Lourdes was President of the Women's Club of our village and she'd get everyone,[the *Bayanihan spirit!*], clean, paint, and decorate with her our small chapel, situated almost at the bosom of the breath-taking mystical Sleeping Beauty in the east where the King Sun never frowns. I still very well remember how happy and accomplished were the faces of the old folks as they made their imprints of their family nomenclatures on the cream walled front fences of the charming House of Prayer of such beautiful, *nagaget* [industrious], *matipid* [thrifty] or *kuripot* [stingy], and religious prayerful people from whom the fiery and brave, horse-riding and *bolo-* wielding Gabriela Silang, one of the Philippine local heroines during the Spanish Regime descended! How I and my siblings excitedly watched too and anticipated the *nuang* [carabao or buffalo] or the *baka* [cow] stopped going around some rare sweet, called locally as *tagapulot,* and the equal rationing of the sweet to each family, with every member holding a *bao* [coconut husk]. But before this main event, the old folks would dance *Manang Biday, Sayaw sa Kalapati* [dove], *Pandanggo sa Ilaw Tinikling,* and other Philippine folkdances in their colourful *patadyong* [national costume for women], and their *Barong Tagalog* [national costume for men], *sometimes on barefoot.* With our parents at the helm of the activities, songs and poetry would then fill the nice cool air coming from the legendary mountain in such lovely evenings of fun and bliss in the 60's and 70's in Rizal, Santa, Ilocos Sur! Those were the days when the village folk and likewise, the townsfolk knew so well the dignity of living from honest toiling and hard work, as early as daybreak to sunset. What joy and contentment bound and united such lovely community and place! All those fun and cultural events had me dreaming more of perfect kingdoms, seemingly, of the utopian vision an innocent child didn't really understand but so wished in her heart! But I would never miss on our great grandfather, *Lolo* Baak who had the most gentle and loving of faces, with the towering height but the years of hard work made him a little hunchback [oh, much lovable than Victor Hugo's "Les Miserables!"], giving him even a more endearing truly adorable countenance to a little girl with his striped blue pyjamas and *baston* sounding like the church bells on a spirited and carefree Sunday morning. *Lolo* Baak, with those big sharp eyes, was a very intelligent but humble man whose wisdom sparkled like diamonds, my ears and heart in awe as he would tell me and my siblings those little secrets and wondrous stories! Oh, how my tender fragile heart would leap and keep every gem of thought and anecdote as I slept and dreamt of hidden worlds [inside mountains and caves, underneath the rivers, oceans, and volcanoes, even on huge tree trunks, giant sea shells, humongous roses, mushrooms, big colourful Spanish fans, and on top of beautiful clouds!]. One day, I asked my parents if it was possible to put up a bridge over China Sea and how they laughed! Indeed, *Lolo* Baak's stories totally fascinated the child in me, including his humorous tales of him and his sons, our "English language-obsessed" *lolos* would each prepare for a dive in all bravado [to each his own daredevil's cry or shibboleth in Ilocano, Tagalog, or fine English!] in that raging deep yet exuberantly elegant Banaoang/Abra River, with the good luck to see a beautiful *serena* [mermaid]in the underworld! Oh yes, there were many tales of mermaids coming from the river when there was an eclipse or whenever it was full moon, and they would have feet to mix with the locals, always with long black hair, and rarely, with the blonde[!], perhaps those times, the *serenas* were one hundred per cent Asians, with no or little cross breed and intermarriages yet, or maybe, the Marilyn Monroes hadn't thought of swimming into the Pacific! Whenever the bus or jeepney would pick up a woman with long hair nearby Quirino Bridge, I'd be ogling her in disbelief and amazement, with everyone doing the same! But oh, some had kinky hair too and dark or black in complexion! Our parents would explain those beautiful friendly mountain people are the *itneg* [Negritoes!]. How the tribal people impressed and fascinated me with their unexploited uncorrupted beings and perfectly white teeth though I just couldn't give up the sweets and the cheese like my good allies, the talking golden mice of granny's wonderful *baul!* The old folks would likewise claim that *Barrio Nagpanawan's* Church, including its belfry, was then buried in the deep river, that every now and then, people, allegedly, could hear bells ringing from underwater, and how I'd prepare my eardrums to bask in such delightful music of the waterworld! Upon the death and burial of our *Lolo* Baak, the entire big clan of Tejadas went to the river, chanting their prayers with their tears to send away all his clothes on a raft, with me wondering if ever those clothes would get to mainland China or even Taiwan as they said these countries are nearest neighbors to the Philippines! Everyone proceeded then to a mountain spring where I thought the fairies and the elves talked with the friendly giants [the cute Titans!], while the muses and nymphs sang as everybody seemed to be talking in many strange tongues while they frolicked in the sparkling waters! *Malambing* [sweet-tongued!] Iloilo was there, so was affectionate Mamburao, joyful Caloocan was there too, including the more cosmopolitan Project 2, of course, high-pitched fiery Ilocos, and so fascinatingly to a child, the great new world, America, and our father's marvelous Great Britain! The setting for multilingual and multicultural exchanges as well as *langue and parole* experience was perfect[!], the uncorrupted mountain springs! Indeed, our childhood didn't just pass unnoticed; it was a perfect time of clean fun, joyful bliss, and lots of adventure with treasure chests of tales and legends and oh, the crazy but delightful and well, scary meal-time English lessons, as well as those love stories! The fondest was the intensely suspenseful night our first cousin came home by surprise from the United States. *Manong* Honesto, fresh from UCLA [!], with his huge luggage I thought they had dwarfs inside who also spoke strange[!], chose a wife that unforgettable so exciting evening from the seated *barrio* girls, and our granny, be-spectacled *Lilang* Isya, in her glittering black *patadyong ken sapaton,* with her long *tabako* like smoking gun, was the one who literally made the pick! Oh God, how everyone was gripped in excitement and suspense as she scouted for the pretty bride from among the nervously dreaming and blushing bevy of our village virgins! Then the loud cheers which almost brought the house down upon her pick of the expectant but shy damsel! Thereafter, *Manong* Honesto and his brand new ecstatic lovely fiancée would take me with them on their big bike while going around the village! Oh, our childhood was in no way a bit of forlorn, monotony, and dullness with all those songs, the poems, and the dances of *amores,* of blanket-weavers, of carpenters, farmers, and fisherfolk, of noble men and women, whether on barefoot or in their stilettoes and well-shined moccasins that came in classic black and in chocolate brown, not to mention the soft and loud prayers that were either chanted or simply recited or even with megaphones and amplifiers[!], with candles glowing in the dramatic dark during the evening processions whenever it was the *barrio fiesta,* the Feast of *Kristo Rey* [October 30th and in one of these evenings, my cousin Vicky and I had our first ghost experience, with her paternal aunt, *Auntie* Lucia, who was just buried then, literally talked and scolded us for getting ice candies from their fridge while everyone was in the procession! How we froze and squeezed ourselves in that big refrigerator as her ghost put off the lights, dragged her *sapaton,* and continued lashing on us until we gathered strength to run towards the church, crying and shouting to everyone for help! Of course, no one believed us!], or during effervescent Sunday mornings as belfries rang the bells like they were divine cymbals, all praises to the most glorious High! What perfect life, what perfect world, and ah, what lovely frills and laces of memory! Yes, to us, to me whom the bell extolled miraculously and so magnanimously in those times and seasons of beautiful smiles, excited sinews, fun and bizarre exhilarating adventures, as well as of exquisite fantastic and even fantabulous dreams! For did I not try then to climb the school bell itself, wanting to discover its mystery, almost losing my dear life at that tender dreaming age of eight, when blue roses were just too radiantly beautiful!

## MY WILD RARE BLUE ORCHID, my *Manang* ERLEEN

"Hey, Mili, what are you up to this time?" My older sister Erleen thunders behind me but her glow and delicate beauty mesmerize even more the little sister's adoring eyes. *Manang* Erleen has always looked so different among bevies of sweet giggles and virginal blooms. Her natural beauty is of an unexplored forest, of some mysterious wilds, so I secretly would call her in my fairy tales as My Wild Rare Blue Orchid. The Hispanic genes and blood complement very well with the fiery yet humble but noble Ilocano spirit and temperament, the Filipino heart and soul.

I try to hide my immaculate but conniving sheets from my sister's prying pretty big hazel brown eyes but she's always quick as the hands of time that was why *Mamang* loved to bring her along in the wet market of Vigan for she'd never complain of the stench of the sea and the dismal litter of unmindful humanity. Her beautiful fair hands would just willingly carry the delicious burden of a big family table of fresh salad, chicken and pork *adobos, tinolas, pinakbet, sinigangs*, pocheros, leche flans, preserved mangoes and sweet pineapples, always with all kinds of bananas especially the *tumok* [cavendish], *saba, senorita, at lakatan,* and sometimes with those red and green apples, sweet lanzones, and oh, the *Pinoy balot* [duck egg] *at penoy* from the city whenever *Papang* travelled for seminars and conferences on how to stop all those unfriendly insects from crawling into Philippine plants and crops. Yes, *Manang* Erleen is the direct contrast of our rather moody, impatient eldest, *Manang* Eloida "Baby Lou" who looks every inch a *chinita* [chinky-eyed]and at times, some mystic beautiful Hebrew especially when she'd tell us the horrors of her mysterious dreams that one night, when we, children were left on our own with our cousins, Obong, Anit, Ibiang, and so little Imiang, *Manang* Baby Lou sent all our wits to the witch as she jumped from her double deck with her eyes burning like those of the classic old English sorceress in fairytales, her voice that of a horrifying hag, so cursed, so damned, and so wretched in a terrifyingly woeful and sickening cave, her hands and long red nails stretched and pointed, ready to attack a small soft and rounded belly of banana and *camote* cues! Oh, we all scampered for the front door and screamed like the begging souls of hell that our *Manong* Junior, a good-looking crushable first lieutenant in the Philippine Army [Oh, they said, he had a lot of those convent-bred fans, and adored as well by the young novices!] came running to us with his loaded rifle, all set to fire on the enemy or legion! Jesus, the lieutenant with often too clean fingernails[How I loved to scrutinize those unbelievably clean soldier's nails!], and the sixteen year-old instant sorceress wrestled on our shocked and disgusted tiles in the living room of an almost perfectly Spanish Senora while the little thin and fat playful but horrified angels watched in fright and in awe for the extraordinary experience of a lifetime one dark quiet night! The oil lamps, and the fireflies versed their mirthful wisdom while the crickets were unaffected in their infinite serenades as the bamboo trees swayed with the cool air in their natural grace, thankful for the full moon and the stars that watched everything in serenity and calm recompense the horrific and hilarious episode of adventurous innocent youth, mostly orphans! But soon, our dashing First Lieutenant cousin in the Phippine Army would then be ambushed and shot by the rebels in Sulu, Mindanao, with me again receiving the news as I'd love to play as well by the *araucaria at bua* [betel nut tree] near our front gate! I was in Grade Four but that RCPI telegram sent the tears and sobs to the young girl's fallen world as she adored the very handsome, very neat, and very kind young lieutenant! Everyone did, and *Auntie* Maura just couldn't stop from her wailings and grief as *Manong* Junior was her favorite nephew who lived with her family for most of his life! His parents, the very *mabait* and excellent cooks, Uncle Sidro and *Auntie* Pinang lived in Tuao, a very far place, almost near Aparri, Cagayan where the crowing of the cock is allegedly heard in Taiwan and vice versa [and I used to wonder as a child if the roosters had the same crowing sounds, or did they also say, cock-a-doodle-do, or just the dialectal *kak karauk ken tar-tarauk*!]. The nice decent Army Major of few words came with his two trucks of men, all young and good-looking with that familiar high cut that the village damsels powdered their faces more like they were performing in the *kabuki*, smelled like the daisies and *rosal*, and were freaking out everytime those fine soldiers smiled or winked at them! They stayed for a really amazing two weeks [with the handsome Philippine Army Major staying in our little guest room, I could smell his fascinating all-too masculine cologne!], with some telling me and their now girlfriends their tales in the war or battle [while chewing gums, smoking their cigars, or holding their long rifles!]. I was a very curious nine year-old girl with little questions that the soldiers became fond of me. They would even shed their tears as they recounted their ordeals but then would flash their biggest smiles when they talked of the abundant fruits of Mindanao and the good locals with their rich tradition and customs [that in the decades to come, I'd exalt all the world's soldiers in my English and Literature classes! This I would do in particular at the Philippine Military Academy [PMA] when I thought of applying as an English teacher in the country's top military school, using the poem, "A Song For Soldiers" as my springboard lesson plus the painting, *Hapag Ng Kainan* which sent the men[all high-ranking officers!] in uniform real sentimental, so touched, and shedding their tears! Unfortunately, they seemed to suspect I was some communist, they wanted to put me to another round of interrogation as panel interview besides in my unforgetfulness and indiscretion, I told them then I had some relatives from UP planting *camote* in the mountains! But most hilarious was when they had to telephone the military guards to stop our taxi as I accidentally and excitedly put all their whiteboard markers in my huge Barbie pink pencil case, and they claimed they were operating on very minimal budget! However, the panel chair soon discovered my husband was a UP Diliman professor and he was so apologetic for reminding him much early on not to approach the interview room! Well, he would then request my husband to get his son a nice male dormitory right in the Diliman campus!]Oh, this experience would then trigger my love and fascination for history especially of wars, great soldiers, and great leaders that I'd do even much better in this subject, *Araling Panlipunan* [Social Studies]than English, perfecting all the quizzes and the long tests that would send our teacher, *Maestra* Liza so grumbling and rumbling in another section for their failure to do the same! In high school, I'd usually get the high marks in the same subject which was why my father told me to major in History [though I also wanted Philosophy, Literature, and Journalism!] when I first enrolled at the University of Santo Tomas [UST]. At freshman year, I would then try to read and research on the more controversial issues, making me all the more sleepless at night! Oh, I thought World History could even make superheroes, and that I could be one! I guess I'd then developed the messianic syndrome! My History professor in UST, Dr. Matias would ask me a barrage of questions covering several chapters of our textbook, with me thinking that was his punishment for my frequent tardiness to our early morning class of seven. My chronic insomnia [that started so early in life!], and hunger for history would oftentimes put me in the hot seat! Well, my fascination for World History somehow helped me cope with my college ordeals, feelings of angst and alienation, my evolving psychological state as I felt multiple personalities were manifesting in me[!], for there were plenty of such movies that time, my "secret gifts," my fears, and living far from home! One day, a good speaker in the university talked of ethics and the plight of soldiers, and so I asked, with my brand new boy's [seven!] haircut, if it was morally acceptable for them to masturbate as Abnormal Psychology claims that's perfect in war time [at the back of my mind, the exquisite hanging heuristic on whether the religious are but exception to the rule as the jerboa whispers of numerous and splendid *papayas* on holy tables especially at breakfasts! *Papaya* is believed to be a turn-off for sexual proclivity!]. My Theology professor was shocked and covered her mouth. Well, I was a college freshman, with a growing penchant for existentialist philosophy, and was very curious of the morality of the world and if ever psychology [oh how I froze in Ma'am Noblejas's class but I adored her teaching method and her on-the-spot graded recitation perhaps due to my masochistic tendencies!] and its psychoanalysis or even psychiatry reconciled well with prevalent social mores[I was reading a lot at the time, my older sister's books at the rooftop of our dormitory along the busy P. Paredes while medical students would be likewise reviewing for their board exams! And oh, they all loved me as I was also selling them all kinds of lotion [for my extra allowance as my five other siblings were all in private schools just like me!] for their expensive skin! Life's early irony!]. But another Theology professor was giving me her two thumbs up for the question I raised [thinking it was relevant!] to the stunned priest who then relied of course on Freud before the books of St. Thomas and the sacraments for his unexpected extrapolation of religion, psychology, philosophy, and ethics. However, I was given a final grade of 2.75 or 79 in the subject. I would then finish college lacking a point zero five per cent to the Latin honors, disappointing my father as I promised him to do much better in college than in my secondary education, which was a time of tree climbing and tree reading for me of the romances, Hemingway, and even Nazi, Germany [as Reader's Digest had plenty of articles on it besides the thick book shared to me by my sister's cool *Atenista* boyfriend!]! But of course my inherent distaste and obstinacy to follow rigid test directions would also either give me the A's or almost the F's. Instead of using academic exposition, I would then be stubbornly answering in crude poetry or some kind of awkward memoirs and crazy letters, upsetting many of my professors but a few exhorted my nonsense before my angry disgruntled classmates! Well, at least, I earned my Bachelor of Science in Education, [BSE], English Major in 1984. I shifted to English on sophomore year as I got overwhelmed by the excellence of my English professor, the late Mrs. Teresita Cendana[sister-in-law of then Minister of Information, Greg Cendana]who'd read Shelley to us in the most crisp, so elegant, and perfect model of Philippine educated English [but of course, I've always preferred it with the *saluyot, katuday ken boggoong*! I would then be checking the length of my tongue compared to hers [as my Speech professor claimed the longer one's tongue, the more flexible and dynamic it is for English!], making my sister, Erleen break into guffaws. I hadn't the slightest idea that she was classmates at the time with the man who'd make my world go round and round much less but more than perfect than Jules Verne's "Around The World In 80 Days" in the years to come!

"Jesus Christ, you are a strange girl, really! Why are you copying the Holy Bible?" *Manang* Erleen makes a nervous laugh and shakes her lovely head as she struggles to squat with her long slender fair and spotless unblemished legs beside me.

"*Eh*, it's the book of Jesus! *Lilang* says it has all the best tales! *Mamang* also used to whisper to me the words here have magic! Or, did she say, miracles? Ah, what's a miracle again? Come on, tell me please!" The girl in green jersey shorts and tiny sleeveless floral blouse in the hues of bright blissful summer now peeves her older sister with the familiar question of women in their nice long veils of delicate unmistakably feminine lace of piety and sobriety as they whisper to each other's heavily perfumed and curious ears during the Holy Mass of our big, bald but highly respected parish priest who'd celebrate the Eucharist in Latin, with his huge back upon the handsome people of *Barangay* Rizal while his outstretched large hands held up high to the Holy Altar of *KRISTO REY* [Christ The King], and his profuse perspiration all visibly falling from his wide forehead. Yes, Fr. Banong celebrated all the Holy Masses in the Roman tongue in our little chapel of chocolate brown and beige with warm yellow, and sometimes, fiery orange in my praising and praying little almost drooping eyes, and these were perfect occasions for the little girl to wallow in the fantasy and greatness of a once most powerful of the Romance languages! Indeed, I was a child but my tiny ears were fascinated by the strange words and dramatic prosody [homiletics] of the queer priest who never smiled but whose hands were always held up high and opened wide[his nonverbal missionary linguistics!] before the beautiful altar of the most good-looking *Santo Kristo* and oh, so perfectly beautiful, *Inang Maria* [Mother Mary] so adorned by fresh and sweet flowers that grew in the charming amiable and charitable gardens of happy wives, strong and brave widows, as well as content spinsters resigned joyfully to their fate, except that all would curse in those Ilocano fiery tongues if those little feet trampled on the delicate stems, and when those chubby mischievous hands uprooted in their nice earthen pots the delicate roses in pink, orange, and yellow with some, in rare white.

"A miracle is when Mama Mary or Jesus appears to fortunate children, oh favoured children!" *Manang* Erleen laughs as she tells her little sister what she herself heard from their old folks. In time, the curious little girl would carefully study that black man nailed on a huge cross [*Santo Kristo*] that hung in a little prayer room under their wooden staircase, whispering to him if he was to do any miracle, and asking when he'd ever come down, then she'd welcome all the religions in the world in their home, listening patiently in her Indian war girl clothes to their sermons, lectures, teachings, beatitudes, including their promos. As if she really understood, yet, it was queer, as queer as her daily hobby and habit of rewriting the sacred verses in her crooked strokes and on her precious bond papers her father would generously and thoughtfully bring her home from work. Good that there was usually a can of FITA or plastic of MARIE, and Sunkist Juice. Sometimes, she'd even offer the churches her Ovaltine! Her guests were more than impressed and grateful, and her granny, puffing her *tabako,* would mumble and say incoherent words in delight, watching her eight year -old grandchild entertain and "engage" the churches in their sunlit *sala*.

## OUR LADY OF FATIMA AND THE LITTLE INDIAN WAR GIRL

"Millie, you will be Jacinta!" I don't remember anymore the beautiful interesting woman [could be our mother!] who assigned me as one of the "three visionaries" of Our Lady of Fatima during our *barangay's* celebration of the Feast of Our Lady. I was just too excited to play the role but was also quite too scared to fail and disappoint [like how I fidgeted on our village's stage when I forgot the steps of our zestful graceful beat, "Pearly Shells" during the Barrio Fiesta that I just danced like a frightened frog[!], and the old folks had such real big but nice laughs!]as again, the entire village would be there to witness and ogle three little children execute the venerable saintly act on barefoot from the meek Chapel to *Pedco* [boundary between Barangay Rizal and Barangay Sacuyya Norte, that produces the best *bolos* in our town!], then back to the brown and beige House of Prayer, one dusk of April [in the 70's]. The very fair and pretty, quite popular, half-American, *Manang* Rosa Borzon was to be Lucia [the oldest of the three favoured ones, who, my brother, Elrey would later woo and serenade, his big flying motorbike during daytime on a standstill [!], with his long brown hair gently blown by the evening air, and his rugged boots more than confident! Oh my brother really looked like a full-blooded Spanish senorito, singing and strumming his guitar right in front of our village chapel at the middle of the night, with the full moon and the stars so envious for the oozing romance that I tried to sketch that moment in my very young heart![However, my brother would later marry the Ambassador's, then Philippine Ambassador to Japan, granddaughter, the very fair and bubbly, Grace Africa Edrosa.]. And was it my Grade One best buddy, Johny Advincula, the brown round chinky-eyed cutie who could have been Francisco? I'm not very sure and confident now of this detail as the years have rubbed off much of the brunt of cosmopolitan existence upon my memory. And little Johny has been long gone to Hawaii [where the first waves of Ilocanos/Filipinos migrated or worked as sugarcane planters like *Hawayano* Uncle Angel, husband of very prayerful *Auntie* Maura, she'd pray the Holy Rosary a dozen times every day and would hear mass also every single day that the old folks would claim her enormous faith and piety helped her earn heaven's favors, hence blessing her a *Hawayano* and a large concrete and fine wooden house!]. Ah, Johny was my best friend and little partner of adventurous innocent crimes [!] as the two of us would buy from a little store inside Banaoang Elementary, dozens of white rabbits, vivas, chocnuts, and *tira-tiras*, paying all these with pebbles then would run as fast as the cheetah, with him always behind me as he was indeed a round and heavy cutie pie! But I vividly remember the joy in that heart of a seven-year old, filling the shoes of Portuguese Jacinta with whom and two other lucky ones the Blessed Mother showed herself on a nice tree while they were attending to their sheep in the fields of Portugal in 1917, asking the world to pray constantly the Holy Rosary for the repentance and conversion of sinners. It was wartime [WW1]when these apparitions of Mother Mary took place. For me, it was a time of child's play, strange dreams or encounters? The unresolved mystery though the heart keeps the secret…I was eight…

"*Nagpintasen!* Oh, what lovely dress! So dainty! So fragrant! Oh, those blue roses are the most beautiful!" She extends her little dirty hands to touch the immaculate transluscent blue dress. Ah, there's nothing like "touching" that perfect dazzling blue dress!

The woman smiles. Her face is so gentle. The sun was high. The little girl was rolling herself on the damp ground as a nice little stream flowed through the big and little stones, the flowery shrubs and the prickly reeds, the thorny willows and the friendly ones. As usual, she was playing by herself with her imaginary friends at the family backyard of all kinds of fruit-bearing trees, what with an agriculturist father who went to Cambridge U. to specialize in Agronomy, and who'd cap his foreign studies with the seeds of the great land in his attache case as he boarded boeing 747 back to the Philippines, and a Home Economics Major of a *mestiza* mother with the long natural curls and golden brown tresses who loved to inspect early, with her bright clothes, nice floral hats, matching gloves and boots, the family pineapples if they were now ready for harvest so she could make them into her delectable fruit-preserves that guests would love to taste, their praises and compliments would make heaven blush and pretend not to hear plus a dutiful loving grandmother who'd tell grand stories of plants and fruits, insects and friendly animals that talked and spoke in the spiritedness, bubble, wit, and wisdom of *Lilang* Ninay, *Mang* Ben, *Tata* Luis, *Tata Hesus, Tata* Mitring, *Nana* Erling, *Maestra Corrong, Maestra* Zeny, *Maestra* Lita, *Maestra* Esteling, *Maestra* Felisa, *Maestra* Tinay, *Maestro* Resting, *Nana* Linda, *Nana* Sabel, *Nana* Lydiang, and *Ninang* Erping, the familiar faces and familiar voices in our village. Oh, granny was such a terrific story teller, with all those spectacular fables and her knack for witty prosopopoeia!

Oh, the eight year-old had a lot of imaginary friends and foes, fascinated by the old folks' tales of American Indians like the noble Cherokee, plus the classic black and white films her parents would choose to see for the big family. One "colored" movie though that made such an imprint in her memory was that of a terrifying dragon that blew from its mouth such big orange and red flames, the eyes also burning, everything set on fire by the horrifying monster that she buried her face on the popcorn! However, she'd then play in their backyard slaying that imaginary horrible monster with her bow and arrow. Then, a real encounter or daydream of the most beautiful woman in a blue dress? A fantasy or imagination of a child who so loved to play alone for some "strange" moments in the orchard of a devout and happy Catholic home? Was it a fairy godmother? But did she have that magic wand? Was it her *Mamang Lourdes,* the beautiful Spanish-Filipina? Was it her mother calling her to lunch? But did she have that dress? Was it a vain ghost who loved to diet with fruits from the seeds of England? Did the beautiful woman step out from the stories and tales of her excellent storyteller of a very loving granny? Or, could it have been a real dream as the little girl then fell asleep in that "radiance," with the soothing fluttering of Indian Mango leaves nearby as the gentle wind blew sweetly its riddle upon that piece of land where fourty-five years later would be the home of two lovers until eternity with the man's tomb faithfully guarded by the same trees?

That perfectly dazzling beautiful dress in the hue of clear blue skies and deep blue waters, and that radiant face of such a lovely gentle woman seemed an eternity to dispel in the memory, fantasy, or dream [?]of a little Indian war girl. How child's play can be so bafflingly mysterious as those years! That became a secret to keep for fear of what it really was, especially to a child who'd often whisper to the holy *Apo Lakay* when He'd ever show or make a little miracle for her as she envied those favoured Portuguese little shepherds besides her indescribable attraction and fascination to delicate church veils of pious women like her mother, granny, aunts, and the women of Ilocandia. That memory was just too overwhelming for an eight year-old! However, after their mother's death in 1972, she became even more "queer" in playtime as she'd copy every day the Holy Bible while she couldn't even read or write very well in the English alphabet though her Grade 2 teachers would admire her reading skills! And of course, listening to the religions of the world while sitting on a can of biscuits! Odd indeed.

By the time she was paraded in the Municipality of historic Vigan on a float of giant and miniscule vegetables and all sorts of local fruits, with her only and older spoiled brat brother, Elrey as escort at this time [1972, constantly reminding the very young First Princess to smile and wave to every *manang ken manong!*], and their younger sister, cute Ely, as her little damsel, the playful little girl of about eight years old seemed to have completely forgotten of that strange dream or odd encounter [?] at the middle of a sunny day. But before she volunteered herself [as in she literally raised her hand, making their pretty mother so overwhelmed with joy and pleasant surprise!] to take the place of her incredibly beautiful older sister, Erleen [who, that rare time refused to ride on that float with all the earth's produce!], as the Princess of the Bureau of Plant and Industry, DA, Region 1, she was first the lucky child bystander during the big fiesta of *Ciudad Fernandina*/ Vigan who was randomly picked in a huge crowd by a ritual dancing *macho guapito* in Igorot *bahag* [Mountain Province local costume for the male], and put on her little neck a huge bright garland of the famous Everlasting [Evergreen!] of the City of Pines [Baguio City], with one big peck on her shy red cheeks! Oh, how her Castilian *Mamang* made exhortations then of her lucky stars and good fortune in a future that was to come after historians would have resolved if the national hero, Jose Rizal ever sired the Aryan despot [as many would speculate and heretofore!], and at a time when scientists would have given sound proof of UFO's and life in Mars! She then grew up reading "The Third Reich" and Lindberg plus Amanda Earrhart [Oh, how I wanted so much to go a-sailing in Tennyson's shallop over the Vermuda Triangle to rescue my heroine!] in junior high school on fragile boughs of the *sarguelas* [Spanish Plum tree]. Her beautiful mestiza mother succumbed to brain cancer a month after the little Indian war girl rode on the float of the best agriculture in the Ilocandia Region, with all the *tarong* [eggplants] perfect for the mouth-watering *poki poki* [grilled eggplants], *kabatiti* [patola/gourd], *kamatis* [tomatoes], *parya* [bitter gourd], *marunggay* [malunggay/horse tree], *tumok* [cavendish], *langka* [jackfruit], *bayag* [Spanish violet plum], etc. etc. etc. Lourdes Pimentel-Batin died on February 11, 1972, leaving six little children to the care of her devastated husband, and her crying doting mother as she was her only child. The little Indian war girl had a pink lollipop rolling in her mouth when her mestiza mother breathed her last, on the Feast Day Of Our Mother Of Lourdes, namesake and special devotion of the Hispanic goddess. Her father was on the hospital floor with a river of tears in his vermillion red shocked eyes with *Auntie* Ilay, his first cousin, carrying his head of dolorous woe while her granny was wailing and fainting three or four times beside the bed of her now lifeless daughter. The rest of the now older orphans were sobbing on the chests of sympathetic women, our relatives, and my two younger sisters, Ely, and Estela Marie who was barely three years old, struggled to imitate their older siblings, stealing glances on everyone, when to cry and when to stop. The girl of eight years in the sun and open fields could not help but keep the details of the sad unfortunate episode in her memory and young heart. She wished this scene was just one of her bad strokes on her sketch pad. Her lollipop had no taste but sour questions like, why is everyone crying, *Lilang* falling here and there with our aunts and uncles catching her on her left and on her right, *Papang* sullen ill on the dirty floor, his head like soccer ball, seemingly waiting to be pitched and thrown at the opportune by spinster *Auntie* Ilay, and why is *Mamang* lying so cold and stiff on that bed of white linen, and she's got no warm loving words for me? The girl began to chronicle at a tender age of eight the seconds and minutes of extreme lamentation, mourning, and grief of her big family which used to have the loudest, the nicest, the best laughter in town, with their home adjudged as the ideal for being colourful, spic and span, keeping nice big and small, regular pets [cats, dogs, rabbits, turtles], and strange ones [monkeys and baby snakes!], with lots of fruit trees, green leafy vegetation [amazing verdure, amazing green!], and all of the lovely blossoms plus all those shells and stones from the sea and wherever in such corner of Paradise! She then would witness, hours later, with her younger sister, six year-old Ely also with the almond eyes, the sudden flow of a whitish liquid coming from the nose of their beautiful mother while she laid on a hospital stretcher in the master's bedroom of their bungalow after she was embalmed in that house she so loved to keep chic and handsome as early as daybreak when her roses, orchids, *san vicentes, gumamelas, santans, rosals, daisies,* and *sampaguitas* would just be too shy but so willing to be kissed by the morning fresh dew. The very fair half- Spanish Senora [Miss College of Education of Far Eastern University [FEU] Manila during her Junior year!] bade her last farewell in her light pink gown she wore on the night her fourth child was crowned First Princess of Vigan, Ilocos Sur, with the best but foreboding [as in the last hoorays!] firecrackers display [!] in January 1972. Her five daughters then wore satin and cotton black dresses and black veils of tearful lace [Oh, how the all black spell bound the adventurous little girl!] while her only son wore a small black and gray suit that seemed to choke him by the neck [!]; the eight year-old curious girl with the drooping but very black eyes counted the wreaths of flowers and they were twice a dozen of sympathies and words of compassion, to comfort and to console the young handsome widower who just received then his TEN OUSTANDING GOVERNMENT EMPLOYEES OF THE PHILIPPINES PLAQUE in Malacanang Palace, from no less than the singing First Lady Imelda Marcos [a soulful singer especially when she'd belt out, *"Dahil Sa Iyo"*] from Leyte, where General Douglas MacArthur made his historic WWII speech, "I shall return." The six orphans were hushed hushed by their *Auntie* Maura, with her daily morning bowls of hot hardboiled eggs, salt generously sprinkled in haste on each white shell with a crack of both sarcasm [why death came so early to her young pretty sister-in-law!] and pity [for the six innocent but playful orphans!]. The wake was in a full two weeks, with the constant burning of wood and coal outside the small front gate, believed to drive away the devil and so, he couldn't steal our mother's beautiful soul[!], yes, just excuse Lord her Castilian cursing in bad times[!], the embers and ashes adding to the wailings, the nervous and quick movements of dozens of *aunties* and uncles, *lolos* and *lolas,* the conservative with so many *pamahiins* [superstitious beliefs like no sweeping of the floor, no *paligo,* no laundry, no tears to fall on the coffin, no meeting and escorting of guests or sympathizers, no bringing home of food, not even candies! Well, I had them in my pocket!] or the more sophisticated [with the American twang in maxims, poetry, and proverbs!], and the sober whispers of elegant men and women who carried flashy handbags on their delicate shoulders or just in their well-lotioned hands with those scarlet red fingernails, the best lavender orchids completing their poise and felicity. They also came, the bureaucrats, the politicians, sculptors, and painters with bottles of wine and the local *basi*, as well as the common tao and the beautiful old folks of our village, who came in to pray, chant, and chat, blaming the tall *araucaria* or the *calachuchi* plants in our front garden as the bad luck or omen of misfortune, or pointing the blame on a supposed witch in the *barrio*, an old woman [who, allegedly transforms into a wild pig or scary crab at night!] whose family lived so close to the mountains and whom our beautiful *Mamang* turned down when one morning she came to sell her the mountain berries! That alleged witch and her family would then just fade away in the memory of the village folk in the many years to come! Some would also put the blame on the insects in the farms that could have bitten our mother and thus, gave her the virus in her brain. Oh, they had so much to whisper to one another's eager ears while sipping Nescafe' in colourful plastic cups, and dipping more than several sunsets their round or square or rectangular biscuits from cans and cans of family and friend-donations. Candles, likewise, seemed countless and tireless as their wicks would just disappear in a wink, then came back in full force, almost setting ablaze the habit of our huge parish priest, this time not with the Latin Romanesque, but with the vernacular, especially that the church *hermana* or matron, *Nana* Erping, my sweet thoughtful godmother, would just speak in the local tongue like most of the old folks. When it was time to bury our beautiful mother, the sun was up but it had much more of a scourging and scorching feel, I burned outside, and inside my heart, it felt very different, as if I and my siblings were left on our own in some subway somewhere in Europe or in New York, with all our luggage and the freezing cold, snow oh snow everywhere, pictures and scenes I'd then see in my parents' magazines or in the cinema back in those old days of divine family bliss on Earth. As I bent to kiss for the last time those most loving and fair hands that gave me joyful baths, combed gently my hair, prepared my Grade One cheese and egg sandwiches, caressed my nape, my head, and body when sick, with that glass of Royal True Orange and raw egg [!], taught me how to hold my Mongol pencil, and almost edible crayons, the formalin got into my nostrils and gave my memory the poignant blow of loss though I was still but a child. I knew then that *Mamang* Lourdes was not coming home with us! Her casket was too heavy for my tender youth, and I stepped away, for my other siblings to make their last kiss and last respects. *Lilang* wailed like the pained ostrich for her most precious while *Papang* kissed our mother on her wordless lips, a tear falling with the last leaf of lovers' legend and love's ode. The following weeks would see the orphans, their granny and aunt pulling from the American jeep and dragging to their *sala Papang* Eloy so drunk and wailing after coming from the public cemetery, his 45 pistol in his hand! The London-schooled agriculturist was almost beaten by the untimely death of his very young and beautiful Spanish-Filipina wife. However, when our *Papang* recovered, we'd all be going every weekend to the cemetery, water the beautiful pots of flowering plants, and eat our *baon* of *pinakbet ken adobong manok* by the tomb of our *Mamang* while the sea breeze and the sound of waves breaking on Santa's rocks filled our memories of those hours of our Sundays spent with our dead elegant mother who never failed to visit us after her death by coming in the most fragrant scent of *Sampaguitas* and the poetry of *kadena de amor* especially at midnight. But well, she was also often seen in her pink gown either walking towards our public school at dawn, or simply there in our garden attending to her roses and orchids. Relatives who came to visit us but failed to be around during her interment then saw her fixing chairs in our living room by our glass windows the moment they got off the cranky bus from Tuguegarao past midnight! A flirtatious househelp likewise saw our Castilian Mama outside the second floor windows of our semi-bungalow home standing by the *Sampaguita plants* one late night! Oh these "sightings" of our *Mamang's* lovely ghost would send our househelp packing their bags elsewhere! Our mother would then be immortalized by two perfect stones, one in life size, the other, half bust, by Mata, the local Master sculptor of San Vicente. Children as we were, we'd be so scared at night especially while both statues were still covered in dark blue for almost a month as the parish priest couldn't make it right away for the blessing with too many *barangays* or villages to attend to, maybe so confused with the venial sins and the mortal ones like, is it venial to gossip during the Holy Eucharist, or is it mortal sin to receive the Holy Communion when the couple made love on Good Friday? I used to wonder if priests had super ears [with the world's small and big sins bombarded into those holy ears!] like the cutest elves in fairy tales!

"Lilies Of The Fields,"the Book and the Girl

Today is another intensely hot summer day in Ilocos Sur. It is the twentieth of May 2019. I woke up early with a lot of burden in my head and the crawling hunger in my stomach for decent breakfast. I would have wanted to eat *tinunong bunog*[grilled fresh water fish] and a whole *papaya*, ripened by the good sunlight and the season of grace. But there is just the memory of a girl that used to run free as a bird for hours in the open fields beside and behind their modest bungalow, mostly after their doting mother passed away. As that fond recollection of a simple ordinary playful girl but with little strange dreams she keeps and she sometimes squeals to her older sister, Erleen, comes to the fore of a sentimental day, Ely, her younger sibling jaunts to the pink and gray veranda for an early morning tete'-a-tete' with a year old Arquiza Nicole, seriously studying the face of her fifty-five year-old grandma, vacationing from the city, a lowly struggling unrecognized author, now on leave for good from that prestigious institution which didn't seem to realize fully her point and her pain in her fb posts against medical malpractice with her then five-month old fb literacy! The writing had to wait, for the bubbly chit chat of two sisters obviously fascinated the toddler with an interestingly smart head, attentively listening, and at times, reacting and responding nonverbally like an agreeing or dissenting adult! Oh, was it only yesterday when that little girl with the Beetles' haircut sat on a can of biscuit to listen to her father and his employees discuss the problems of the soil, the plants, and the crops while they sipped on their hot cups of coffee and kept waiting for their precious biscuits? Afterwhich the serious listening would be followed by her scribbling of words, verses, line after line, copying here and copying there of that large book the old folks called the Sacred Scripture or the Holy Bible, its Old Testament, and its New Testament! Then when her fingers were tired, she'd proceed to the open fields to frolic with the huge dragonflies, colourful butterflies, and laughing frogs, chase the sparrows, the ravens, and would run as fast as a rabbit to feel the air on her face, the wind blowing from behind, lifting her small and frail body up the ground for magical moments of fantasy and delight, and going back home with the freshness and candor of a new and happy day, impeccably exciting wild flowers at the back of her joyous tiny ears, and on her little mirthful hands, with all kinds of fascinating reeds and shrubs around her tiny waistline! Her siblings would conspire to escape the caring loving watch of their granny for an almost daily taste of carefree and fun, together with four cousins whose mother, the very pious *Auntie* Maura would usually keep in their big wooden house so as not to injure their knees and elbows with the rashness of youth. Of course, they'd always managed to squeeze themselves to a hole and climb over the fences, and off, the orphans and their cousins chasing one another, either under clear blue skies or under the rains in the great farms and open fields, sometimes, even with the frightful thunder and lightning, unmindful of what the old folks warned as electrocution by fulmination or *"tamaan kayo dyaske ng kidlat!"*

At about lunch time, my niece Alyssa Lourdes brings me a hot bowl of heavenly *dinengdeng* [Ilocano viand]. Oh, the fringe benefits of rural living and proximity of kin's kingdoms! Minutes after, Estela Marie, my much younger sister comes with a bunch of glorious, very white, very pure *umaalimuom/humahalimuyak* [fragrant] *Sampaguita*, the traditional national flower! Oh, how perfect timing for my reminiscence of that growing lass who, at around thirteen, with her hair rollers [!], was reading her first novel on a tree branch, and underneath were bushes and bushes of the immaculate *Sampaguita*! How she eagerly read each page of "Lilies Of The Fields," curious if the stranger ever fell in love [oh, the innate romanticism!] with one of the young and charming nuns as he did his gracious carpentry for their convent at the middle of some prairie [farm!]. Well, I no longer remember the author [though Google says, William Edmund Barrett!] but I give him my grand salute and two thumbs up for the impact of the book and its story in my life, in my heart, and soul, which is quite very surprising and perplexing as I can't even recall the plot except that it talked of the beauty of simple existence in God's divine providence, and trust for a fellow human being, giving a picture-perfect life in peace and of bliss! Maybe the theme just got the daydreaming lass on a tree branch, unmindful of the chameleon slowly climbing underneath the fragile bough. Besides, they claim, first love never dies! That book was my first love of the world of print, not to mention those wonderful textbooks then in Grades 1, 2, and 3! It was magic, still is, as far and as much as my heart and soul could attest and remember! Love, selfless and trusting love for humanity in God's wonderful grace. Simple but more than eloquent!

From then on, the adolescent craved and yearned for more and more of what worlds existed and exist in every magical story of print [like the books of Hemingway, in particular, his "Old Man And The Sea"[providential perhaps that in time, she'd pen biographies of septuagenarians!], George Orwell's "Animal Farm,""The African," Nancy Drew mysteries," J. D. Salinger's Catcher in the Rye!] as she picked and chewed the fresh fruits of her tree reading sanctuaries. The danger of falling and breaking her neck or her head did not matter so much more than her desire to live in so many lives in so many places in so many worlds! Her father all the more kept the embers, their flames, their fire burning by subscribing for his young daughter monthly editions of then very famous READER'S DIGEST [oh, most sacred and precious to that youth, she'd swing to her trees the moment the postman came by the gate!], buying as well local magazines like the BANNAWAG and LIWAYWAY plus dozens of *komiks*, jingles, aside from the broadsheets and dailies, local tabloids, the histories and agricultures of the continents, the philosophies of the ages, their arts, literature, and their cultures, plus the health books and all the religious biblical stories! As if all those were not enough for he would then require his fourth child to memorize every day, at least three to five words from Oxford, and that she should be able to spell and give their meaning as she untied his office shoes from office! Oh, so much for the running and for the wild flower picking while my pimples began to be more than plentiful on my now very conscious adolescent face! There seemed to be less time for more swimming in the river, watching how the Abra River and the China Sea would come together in such poetic magnificence, or just dipping in the family fishpond with my siblings and cousins, together with the tadpoles [!], waiting for the caterpillar to become the most iridescent perfection, having joyrides either on the invented "slides" of *Manong* Rey, or on our individual bikes [mine was a four-wheel low bike, with all the blooms and verdure of the planet!]while John Denver was playing in the air, and chasing the *pasagad* or *karitela* [cart] of *Nana* Tibang, that was always full of young sugarcane and which she'd generously make me catch with my eager hands while her carabao would dart up and down the still rough and rugged inner roads to and fro the rice paddies and open fields! My pimples just would not have enough of my face for they'd grow in number, morning after morning. All the more that I just wanted to read on the Cherries, the Lemon trees, the Guava trees, the Indian Mangoes, the Sarguelas, the Tamarind, on all my trees of comfort and print joy! Oh, when the menstruation came, I wailed so loud just like every girl in our clan [oh, the hilarious tradition of our womenfolk!], with my older brother Elrey sent running to *Lilang* Ninay's *sari sari* store to grab that feminine napkin! How that girl thing terrified me that I wanted to find out more of its mystery in books! I thought Hemingway's novels could help! Thus, my best ally in the sweet cliché, salad days of life, was the print world, aside of course, my wild rare blue orchid who'd read and read to me all those local magazine love stories when I was then much too young to climb the vines and to read on my own. And while the dry and wet seasons came and went with the hands of time, Barbara Cartland and Mills 'N Boon plus Abnormal Psychology[!] would then creep in so preponderantly enthralling to my psyche that as the *kariton* [cart]peddlers would camp almost thrice a year by our Grotto of Our Lady Of Lourdes, or by our village church, I'd be interviewing the very intriguing interesting folks a la Freudian, and bantering with them vis-à-vis my ecstasy and angst over the fate of the unlikely or unexpected lovers of the romance of the moment, with the betel nut rolling on my tongue as we had a lot of the *bua by our front small and big gates!* I would then dream of my own prince charming that I'd be singing while *nagsasaing* [cooking rice in the pot!], and our granny, too keen with the *pamahiin,* would say, "*Apo ko,* someday, you'd marry an old man!" "Well, as long as he'd look like James Bond, why not?" I'd secretly muse to my naughty self as dishes were washed with pure clean bursting water and youthful enraptured bubbles! And oh, dozens of broken glassware and the china as dreams cascaded through the years to reach One Magical World... "Love and harmony combine, And around our souls intwine, While thy branches mix with mine, And our roots together join."[Blake's "Song"]

## Chapter Three

# Summer Solstice and a Love Story in Up

"*Hoy*, Millie, you've got classes today! Sir's lecturing! *Hala ka!*" Ate Fely brings the good or bad news but well, THE GREAT LEGEND has it that it was the harbinger of my life's ultimate solstice with all the summers of April. I was then a Ph.D. student at the University of the Philippines, Diliman majoring in Language Teaching or Language Education. This was 1992, April.

"Oh my God! Ma'am Lita, bye!" I snatched my floral bag from where it carefully sat and climbed up to the third floor of the Benitez Hall. I was more than two hours late for my summer Elective class, EDL 205 [Second Language Acquisition], and it was the first day! All along I was foolishly thinking there won't be any formal meeting that day although I went to the university much earlier. To kill time and chit chat with the Oblation, the Acacia trees, and oh, with my good friends among the clerks and the personnel [like Ma'am Lita Sangel, *ate* Fely, *ate* Ading, and *tata* Ped Alviar] as I've been studying at the UP College of Education for five years, having earned there my Master's degree in Education in Educational Administration. So, I was more than confident and oh, complacent!

He was lecturing. He was writing on the board while he was lecturing.

His nasal baritone voice echoed. His fine gray glistened with his pomade and his brilliance. I heard him. I knew. My heart went wild. I ran to the back door.

"Yes, Ma'am? Are you enrolled in this class?" He asked, smiling. My heart leaped.

"Oh yes Sir. I am." My voice tried to be normal but it failed. I sounded so nervous that I became even more high-pitched with my Ilocano accent. "Here's my class card *po*." The professor outside Rm. 107 who was then eyeing me during enrolment time while I lined up to drink from the fountain, irritating me then a bit, muttering to myself, "What's wrong with this man?" The same professor who was standing by the door of the Office of Language Teaching, holding the globe [!], and smiling as he was overhearing me request *Mang* Ading, the very helpful and kind secretary, to give me the best professor for my summer class [the egotistic in me! as if I had any single neuron then!]. Oh God, he is in fact my teacher, my summer professor! I was shrinking to the bottom of my shameful queendom!

"Emily? Emily Bronte?" He says, still smiling. Now, the eyes are even more enigmatic, looking right and deep through my soul. The smile makes me fart, oh, softly and discreetly as I've always had those subtleties whenever I'd get excited, this queerness I inherited from my father who chose to bring home all sorts of seeds than those fine sweets from London after his special studies in that land of "The Prince And The Pauper" and the adorable Princess Di [I cried and cried when her limou or was it BMW, crashed at the French tunnels because of fate?]Heaven knows! But her fairytale lived on in my heart, yes, even today as I'm truly, a romantic, and romanticism is my oxygen especially when I'm in the city! Oh, I thought once I was a skeptic or nihilist, Jesus[!], when I failed my Trigonometry in the Third Quarter of senior high school [as I was by this time trying to understand the point of the Third Reich[!], but gee, my NCEE results showed a 99 % in my Math, with an overall performance grade of 99 %! Well, I just got lucky, of course!], and so, I was banned to take the UPCAT [my mother would've turned endlessly in her beautiful repose as UP was her dream for her fourth child, I guess for she'd usually whisper this in my tender ears!]. But destiny would intervene, hence, I got to overcome a bit the postmodern cynicism. The life story of then Living Saint Mother Teresa inspired me so much to listen to the voice in my heart and to find contentment and miracle in simple existence, so I thought one failure could bring forth the fortune out of the mundane! Besides, the essay question [aside from the I.Q. test, oh, I got one? Wasn't very sure!] in the UP COE Qualifying Examination for my M.Ed. had something to do with the Philippine diaspora, so at least I was able to write a couple of paragraphs. I've just read then Bienvenido Santos's "Scent of Apples." Finally, my mother would've kept cool with her Castilian tongue in her tomb, situated at the bosom of the spectacular Ilocos Mountain Ranges and overlooking the breath-taking China Sea!

"Oh no, Sir! It's MILLIE. Millie Pimentel Batin." I correct him fast and emphatically. At this point, the whole class teased and cheered. They sensed something was to begin between the tall dark dashingly handsome UP professor and the oh, not so impressive tardy [notorious?] UP graduate student wearing her favorite faded *maong* [denim]skirt and a Collezione striped dirty white shirt, plus worn out sneakers and a pair of crazy feminine socks. He was fourty-five and she was twenty-nine. The sudden gust of April wind and the golden ray of sunlight passing through the windows of Room 320 threw me into a page of Cartland's best sellers! And thus, I farted in the magical motion of time.

From that first day of class, my life was never the same. Those perfect eyes of a true Adonis beguiled my entire being. They bore with them the secret mystery of a hidden world. They sparkled yet they were humble. They were enthralling but they were pure. They were the eyes of MY DESTINED PRINCE CHARMING! I was totally, absolutely, completely love-struck for the very first time in my life!

And, oh, his hair? There was no other mane like his! He had a kingly, princely, knightly amazingly robust thick and wavy hair that gave justice to every phoneme, every morpheme, every orthography of that universal compliment that comes in a phrase, a noun phrase with several syntagmatic functions but of one semantic interlude of an epithet or metaphor, CROWNING GLORY. Ah, mythical Pegasus was in no way a bit of comparison. I'd then verse such unknown lines of delight with that healthy mass of handsome hair in the sweet nest of great true love for the next twenty four years! O love so glorious, so delightful, immensely beguiling my soul! Nothing else brings such magical rapture...oh but the mane intoxicates every second those handsome strands glow and allure in the memory of my heart!

But, of course, the phase of "getting to know you" and oh, Blake's chariots of fire, courtship!

It's my turn to report in front of the class. Powerpoints and overhead projectors aren't yet the trend but cartolinas and Manila papers. Having just been fired [!]as a high school English teacher due to my philanthropic cause of leading the fight for what our junior group [not gang!]of teachers believed as principled, but which unfortunately got me axed [my idealism, chronic insomnia, and urinary tract as the real culprit! Greek mythology was just the aperitif! And it was never my fault if my high school students went up their seats to greet me one day after they went to see the movie, "Dead Poets Society!" Maybe they just simply loved "Twilight Zone!"], I am quite confident my visual aids are more than ready and sufficient to speak on my behalf, with all my flower vases, and doodles of a humongous shrub, its equally large flowers as the begonia, stalks and leaves more like the rhubarb, opening up unabashedly and gloriously to the clear skies, and a dozen more dramatically crawling down the conspiring ravine, my metaphor and parody for second language acquisition, SLA. Whoa! PROFESSOR ENZO QUIAMBAO QUIAMBAO was thinking of something else!

He just wouldn't let me sit. I could just fart elegantly in disbelief! The topic of his classic persistent probe? My personal life! Oh, the class goes crazy, jeering, and cheering and shrieking mad! The maroon professionals including the sporty and fashionable Koreans, as well as the Thai English interpreter of the soon to be crowned Miss Asia-Pacific, of course, from quintessential Thailand[!], just forget all finesse and ethical conduct, and keep on applauding, pushing and elbowing one another until the good but now wooing professor finally charts back to the map of the academic kingdom, and starts to raise the more relevant questions of the linguistic athenaeum. Of course I prefer much better the first rounds of his heuristics though *Dalagang* Filipina has to be a bit of demure like the unassuming but bewitching masterpiece of the Italian genius. That afternoon in the country's premier state university is forever a fantastic bubbly bursting memory. The handsome intellectual is but a human being. Was...

Oh, the Midterms and the Finals were far from romantic but

nonetheless, they excited me as I prepared very well to satisfy my hubris [oh, Narcissus and my illusionary ivory tower!], and to impress him, Professor Quiambao. The list of items was quite paradoxical to the demands of the arid weather with all those linguistic terms to define, such as proficiency, fluency, and articulation [If your repartee' in English is flawless, does that mean you're fluent? Or, does it reveal your articulation and proficiency but how about if you sounded more your native accent? Oh, the proverbial riddle in ESL and EFL but thanks to the great Hindu linguist, Braj Kachru for his all embracing inclusive and liberating world Englishes, wE![but seemingly quite late in the frame!] ; those theories and methods and techniques of SLA to discuss, critique, exemplify, and oh, venerate! Like for example, is it okay to say, *Halika fr., maglandi tayo* while a woman is clad in a bikini? But then of course sociolinguistics would come in to justify the idiom like again the case of a college freshman claiming she fingers the rice when she cooks for direct translation from Filipino to English! Oh, I tried to beat myself and the ennui of the climate. When the papers were returned, my paper had four to five languages on every possible line and space! The professor was too magnanimous with the feeding back in Latin, Spanish, French, English, and Singaporean English as traces of RELC-Singapore,[Prof. Quiambao earned his Diplomate in Applied Linguistics there with High Distinction, and hence, his admiration for Dr. Jack Richards.] and well, the points. He gave me a 1.0 or an A on both exams, with my Finals bearing not much answer on interlanguage as I thought I'd just draw the crawling *kabatiti* or *patola* [gourd] to explain for the linguistic phenomenon, the authentic way or parlance. I've always loved local symbols for their ingenuity and impact on my sense of being and identity, besides, I felt, it's my language and language experience called for in the situation in context, for didn't I learn first my English while our family were planting the flora [all kinds of plants and herbs and blossoms!] in our backyard and endless gardens and plots as our parents would give us on- the- spot vocabulary and spelling contests while digging through the moist earth with all those crawling tiny and fat earthworms, and some Spanish too, with the cute little curses of our pretty *Mamang* Lourdes that one day, I copied her *punieta!,* and she quickly covered my mouth with her nice yellow gloves, or my father's idiolect of disgust, *laglag* [!]or fool. Oh, my very scholarly and research-oriented professor loved my crawling *patola,* my metaphor for my idiolectal interlanguage that he then gave me a final grade of 1.0 [A]! The behind the scenes story is that Prof. Quiambao steadfastly scheduled my one- on- one consultations with him in between our regular class sessions but which I only was able to attend once before I went home to Ilocos for the Holy Week [as I didn't want to miss the early morning ritual of our *Lilang* and our *Auntie* Maura singing the *pasyon,* in our *sirok*/basement for our granny, while on the second floor of the large wooden house for our aunt!] on Maundy Thursday and Good Friday, oh, actually the entire Holy Week, both of them wearing their long black mourning veils while singing and chanting!] carrying with me his huge precious very new book which I proudly showed to my father who then made a short but mindboggling remark, "Your professor likes you." Well, I wasn't very sure of that so I decided to gift my professsor with a plastic of the best green Indian Mangoes from our backyard, my childhood playground where I'd pee most of the time as our agriculturist father would usually mention that's good for the trees and the flora! Hence, my second conference with my professor was when I got back to the city, knocked at his office door one afternoon, and gave him my *pasalubong* [gift], the old, time and tested Filipino tradition and custom. *Bongga*[wow!], the succulent greens more than appealed to his taste and heart; they sweetly devastated him, his frontline bunks were wiped out. He could not forget the fruit and the woman! Paradise was henceforth regained after so long a time for Enzo Quiambao Quiambao. Master Milton could not have missed, including the agricultural theory of my father, and the nice superstition in our small town that the best way to a man's heart is for him to taste the produce of your backyard with your own body fluids or nutrients, oh!

It was the end of Summer Classes 1992. Diliman was being blessed once more by gentle showers. I was feeling odd; ecstatic and yet quite scared. Professor Quiambao was walking me to Balara for my Katipunan-bound jeepney ride! He held my umbrella to the drizzle, the first of those rapturously magical moments [!], so that my then delirious head won't catch the falling worms from the trees [Oh God, there were so many of those hanging almost invisible parasites on the huge trees in Loyola that the English-speaking elite, the *conyo,* would almost swallow them unawares as they enunciated the lexeme, "comfortably" with silent R[!], not so much of the syllable-timed Philippine English! Oh, Ilocanos excel with the "R" as in bumpeRRR to bumpeRRR for Metro Manila traffic or aRRRmageddon!], and keep me safe from the flu besides of course, he was a man and I was a woman [Feminism and equality could wait, huh!]. We trekked the now muddy pathways behind the College of Education, supposedly a shortcut but it was the longest shortcut I've ever walked! My professor's voice was beginning to sound more like soothing caressing whispers in my obviously tickled ears, his warm body almost desirably crushing mine and my sanity, his hands, oh those hands, were perfect! So big, so gentlemanly, so protective, the texture felt so good, and so promising of unknown delights![I've always been tactile and auditory to complement my vision, my olfactory, and taste buds, unmistakably a real homo sapiens!]. Oh, Diliman was just too unbelievably perfect, glorious, glorious until some lady, suddenly crossed our path and ogled me like I was the main course for the night! She was obviously a fan of the most dashing professor of the country's top university for Sir Enzo would never meet a class without his large library in his head, his charms in his eyes, lips, and manly strides, his goodness and kindness sparkling and overflowing in his greetings, idioms, and exceptionally beautiful, cordial, rich Bulakeno Tagalog, his Filipino, world class so much so that he was then awarded a SEASSI Fulbright Lecturing Grant to the University of Washington to teach the American scholars write their thesis in the Philippine national language as they researched on Asian cultures. From the intercontinental grapevine, it seemed that Professor Quiambao did not fail to wow the Western intellectuals. Except that he was warned by the university security not to shake again the apple trees that surrounded the campus [in the Philippine rural areas, customarily, people would shake the trees, if manageable [!], for the ripe fruits and the edible beetle to fall [!]], where his favorite and idol, Bruce Lee rests in eternal silence [My brother Elrey used to copy his martial arts a lot as well as his trademark sounds! I've always adored his philosophy in much the same way as the great wisdom of Confucius!]. Ah, no one would ever forget Sir Enzo's jokes that could send holy veils and false teeth literally flying in the air, tummies bloating with laughter, jaws and facial muscles more than exorcised, oh, exercised in unexpected instant guffaws! Yes, he does not only teach and inspire, he also tickles all your funny bones, including your heart and your soul! Oh, when the lady could not forestall the shining knight and the naughty secretly giggling damsel, the romance of Diliman continued as the duchess of some neighboring kingdom left in haste for the king and queen of Diliman muds, oh, hearts obviously imparadised their expectant beings in that beautiful fairytale-like drizzly afternoon, unmindful of anything but two hearts bellowing less shamefully passion and unspoken love! The two pairs of feet made more nervous excited steps into the generous accommodating muds and soaked but singing willows of the campus while their hearts "beating each to each"[Robert Browning] kept on exchanging the sweetest words from all of love's exhilarating nectar and rarest honeybee, not noticing that dusk was soon to fall and Diliman would literally become even darker, with eye glasses-wearing Adans and Eves to bask in pleasure in the Sunken Garden, bribing the authorities with their brilliant shibboleths and fiery poesy when caught in all of their divine glory! Balara would then halt the magical walk with its lines of wishful Acacia[Oh, some got axed and chain-sawed years later for road widening!], and the Katipunan ride! I turned to my good-looking professor and said my gratitude, his smile perfect as the most eloquent of sunsets! I hesitantly climbed the waiting jeepney that was almost full of spent humanity. He stood there in the drizzle, so handsome, so unbelievably handsome, but then his enigmatic eyes were on my shoes, on my shoes! I kept waving my hand, and he kept looking down. Humanity suddenly came back to life as it was tickled by both the blushing romance and the humor of the hour! The now fully alive humans giggled as the Filipino pride, *Katas Ng Saudi* [a Philippine colloquial for Saudi Arabian souvenir!] moved, danced, and gyrated like a euphoric overjoyed victorious sheik or a grateful taipan who has just made more millions for his net worth! Dear Lord, my sneakers were full of mud! My pinky socks were also splashed with mud! But then again, my prince charming stood smiling and gorgeously handsome in the rain, and no mud could ever muddle that perfect picture, that perfect portrait of my love!

Professor Quiambao then flew to Seattle, United States of America, around May of 1992. I was taken in by my Alma Mater that gave me my free tertiary education [Scholarship Grant], the University of Santo Tomas [UST] in Espana, Manila, the Royal Pontifical University and the oldest in Asia but where the floods seem to never get antiquated or end. Ma'am Cendana was studying me very closely, wanting to know if I was still the young Thomasian who served as a shy staff writer then hesitant Literary Editor of the internationally published [meant to reach the Holy See, Rome!]Education Journal[EJ], or more now of the typical radical *aktibista o sakit ng ulo[!]*[Philippine colloquial!], from my years of graduate studies in UP [Oh, that's no shocking news anyway as everybody thinks that way!]. Well, it seemed she still liked what she saw and heard in that short interview. I was given a full-time teaching load at the College of Education, with several loads at the Conservatory of Music [Oh, I've never been like Shirley Maclaine but my, how I infinitely adore her!], and gee, the College of Engineering that produces many of the country's and world's best engineers! This was my first taste of college teaching [so, I taught Orwell, and Shakespeare, even Homer [oh yes!] and metafiction in Technical Writing [!] as I enjoyed the academic freedom with my UP professors singing the tunes of *KALAYAAN/* FREEDOM in my head! Well, not much of a big deal, huh!], and my first experience to wade in waist-deep floods while crying in my newly bought very precious stilettoes [as I rarely bought over a thousand pesos!]at six o'clock in the evening, Angelus prayer time! When I finally got home by almost midnight, my clothes and all of me dried up like stringbeans, including my hair[!] from the terrible traffic, my pretty sister served me one giant *alimasag* [blue crab] on her delicate china that I couldn't believe my eyes and threw my wits to the toilet! I then slept like crazy for the first time in my life on my school clothes and the loathesome residue of unpoetic flood that my nightmare had me swimming again and again in those city floods while test papers just won't disappear but kept floating with the red, the green, and all kinds of pen! How I cursed in my nightmare!

August 1992. "Millie, your UP prof. called. *Ikaw ha, bakit ka tinatawagan ng prof. mo? Oyy!"* Ma'am Adviento, my English Coordinator could not hide her fancy and interest. I was dumbfounded! It was unexpected though he told me he'll be ringing me up wherever I was once he got back in the Philippine *Fiesta* Islands. My heart was incontrollably beating fast. When I stepped with my muddy sneakers and socks on that Katipunan jeepney mid May, and he stood there smiling like a prince in the drizzle, there was no real and clear admission yet of anything romantic, or intimate. Everything was just poetic flirtatious nonverbal and electric attraction, of course, UNSPOKEN LOVE in the pretense of delightful intellectual and academic discourse, felicity, and gratitude for the book, the grade [for me], and for the Indian Mangoes [for him]. But now, he's back and he just called. I'd learn later that he got my number from *Ate* Ading as she was in charge of our files. I wasn't able to sleep an hour that night and of course, there wasn't any nightmare! The following day, he called again, and this time around, I was able to receive the call. I just came from my wonderful and engaging Chemical Engineering class where the thesis statement took us almost an eternity to discuss like is it okay to write a paper on nukes [!], or on how to fight steel corrosion, even tooth decay [ouch! Vice Ganda's all-time hit!], and whether the implied is better than the definite to which I retorted, "The better thoughts are always met with a frown!" so I was quite tired but the moment I heard the nasal baritone voice, my world stopped then it spun wildly, vigorously and I was intoxicated with unparalleled joy! I knew then that I was entering a new world, the best there could possibly be! Well, the romantic farting was inevitable but thank God, he was at the other side of the world! *Nakakahiya naman!*[Not so well-bred flirtation, oh!].

He came to UST College of Engineering on September 11, 1992. The budding Thomasian Civil and Chemical engineers eyed him carefully as they loved their twenty-nine year-old professor in Technical Writing who'd make them laugh so hard from time to time with her crazy philosophies and tales, like talking to another jeepney passenger as if he were her best friend only to finally realize after some heart-warming chit chat that this guy is a total stranger[!], or looking for her hard earned pay envelope that she had then thrown in the trash can! Professor Quiambao was wearing powder blue long sleeved-polo, brown pants, and well-shined moccasin. *Ang gwapo! Grabe!* [Real handsome, ladies swoon!]. Oh, I just wanted to hide and to pee, more so, to fart! My heart was already wild, my head swirling, my vision burning! My legs were trembling, my long COD senorita skirt with black lace seemed to fall as my shiny thick black belt could not just suddenly hold! My white blouse with some delicate ruffles and frills [to give me boobs!] felt too small for my nervousness was killing me, my lungs wanted to burst! My black stiletto could not carry an iota of grace that I began to walk like a frightened duck with loose bowel movement[LBM!]. But of course, I excused myself to the Faculty CR, sprayed some cologne

[Oh, my allergies!], brushed vigorously my teeth [like my favorite, Frank McCourt!], put some demure red lipstick on my quivering but eager [oh!] lips in erstwhile earnestness[!], combed my hair and checked if my orange shampoo worked well on my scalp, powdered my face with the Johnson Baby Powder, and recited a short prayer of THANKSGIVING before the amused mirror [Jesus knows I went seeking for succor with a short missive to His holy women in the Pink Sisters Convent and Sta. Clara but I forgot the eggs [the usual offering!] while my apple of the eye was literally shaking apple trees [out of tradition!] at the University of Washington, not so far from the Big Apple!]. As I stepped out of the Ladies Room, my God, his imported Jovan [his all-time favorite!] thrilled my olfactory, and my whole being, and his hair? God, his mane just could not escape my adoring eyes! My fingers itched to touch that perfection of male crowning glory [if only I could pull then even just but one strand! Oh, that naughty witch in me! But, I haven't exchanged thrilling beautiful books on the art of witchcraft yet with my dear brainy eccentric friend, Ren Magsanoc at the time though we'd bump in Diliman more than once!]. Professor Enzo Quiambao Quiambao was every inch a god of Mt. *Apo*. *Si Malakas* of the Filipino epic, and well, I felt I was looking good [*si Maganda*, huh!] that moment from the way he was looking at me! My granny and my sister, Erleen would always remind me then to keep my head, and that seemed to tell me I'd look a little better with my head than with just the face, oh! The truth makes one real hot, my motto! Besides, mirrors often lie when you stand far from them! So, get closer 'til they fall and break!

In Max Restaurant, Recto, our fate of FOREVER was sealed! But that came after I ordered so much food [as if I had money in my purse but then again, I was thinking of the Filipino custom of the man to pay for everything *syempre*! Dutch treat does not work perfectly in the Philippines! Well, I was just really nervous that I thought food would shield me from the overwhelming happiness and extreme excitement my heart could not seem to contain. So, the curious waiter wrote, *kare-kare, crispy pata, bulalo, pancit canton, chopsuey, cream of asparagus soup, and of course,* one whole Max spring fried chicken plus fried rice and two glasses of their finest juice not to forget two glasses more of clean and cold water! Barbara Cartland was all over me, every Mills N' Boon I read was literally coming to life, and I was choking crazy! The young and not so young waiters were whispering to one another as if they were guessing if we could actually eat as maybe, they saw the pink rattle and red ecstasy on our faces and movements, the twinkling stars in our eyes though it was lunch time, aside from how we both smelled; oh, our colognes were beating all their air fresheners [I was secretly itching all over with my allergies! But for love, no fret!]! While I tried to bite the crispy chicken leg the most feminine way I could so as not to turn off the cock, oh the rooster, the dashing handsome man suddenly confessed of his true feelings, and leaving me no second to breathe, he asked, "Emy, do you love me too?" Oh, I almost swallowed MAX! I remembered fast and quick what my favorite brilliant unorthodox UP female professors [Dr. Gaceta and Dr. Arreza] taught us, to be straightforward with the truth, and not mince words! Hence, I answered, "Yes Sir, will you marry me? By the way, I don't have boobs! But you know, I've got a nice plateau!" Enzo could not stop laughing, with tears in his eyes as he reached for my oily hands and kissed them, with the chicken leg left for the plate or some soul to bite, oh! I wanted though to make *pabalot* [not the doggie bag!]of the rest of the untouched food but my heart was bursting with happiness, and so was Enzo who'd then leave a generous tip for the gracious and grateful waiters!

Once the historic love pact was done and accomplished, we decided to see a movie in a cinema right beside Max Restau. I then forgot I still had one more class in UST, with the Music Majors at the Conservatory. They'd later tell me they were more than grateful for my forgetting as they at least got more time to prepare and oil their respective musical organs and instruments for their interpretative performances in our English class. Was it Maugham I was teaching them ["By Force Of Circumstance"] at the time or Frost["Fire and Ice"]? Their culminating event was a spectacular musical play, a la "Midsummer's Night Dream!" Guess what English course I was assigned then to teach them? Technical Writing too but of course, I felt I had to get them write in context so "Aria babes! You have every reason to perform the drama and music of your Technical English!" As for the movie, it had no title, no plot, no story, no actors at all; it just had all the sounds! Dear Lord, I was then kissed for the very first time by my first ever boyfriend! His name was ENZO! Oh, a kiss could not be like any other kiss, sorry Shakespeare! Enzo kissed me to eternity...and I was lifted to the skies with William Blake's most esurient "chariots of fire," the "arrows of desire" deep into my soul, oh, my childhood fantasies turned "burning gold," and hence, my mortal fingers, my mortal hands touched the clouds of heaven! That day was 11 September 1992.

## HONEYMOON MONTHS, The Roads To PARADISE

"Oh, Enzo, what is this place? Are we in paradise?!" I'm shouting and screaming out of joy as my face and body seem to fly with the sultry and pleasant winds, with me almost in a Hollywood action and romance flick, holding on tight at the rear handle of my boyfriend's handsome Silver Beauty, his owner jeep as it speeds along a mirthful stream, along tall friendly willows, Acacia trees, Tamarind trees, the familiar pliant Bamboo trees, Caballeros, the *Ipil-ipil, Kamagong, Camachiles, Bananas, Banabas,* sunlit rice paddies, strutting chewing goats, lazy ducks, pregnant cows, running horses, and beasts of burden busy with the earth, a young lanky Jose or Pedro in charge of the ploughing, and their tired but able elders eating their *baons* with their hands, simple but happy women busy with the baskets of homemade delicacies, their little ones bantering under shady Mango trees. My maroon Cinderella skirt and baby pink blouse wanted to float in the cool fresh air while my shoulder-length loose hair just could not stop prancing and dancing in the pure frenzy of uninterrupted beautiful nature. This was our first official date after our formal admissions and confessions which led to our love covenant on that historic September 11.

Bustos, Bulacan. A heaven on Earth.

Enzo gently reminds me to hold tighter as the rough roads are long; Silver Beauty zig zags here and there, zig zags again in a minute and again and again as it avoids the bigger stones, some bush, some canal, some puddle, then overtakes a small tractor, a yellow fiera of *takong/inahin* [mother pig], fully loaded carts of sacks of grains, of rice, of corn, of men, women, and children wearing on their faces and in their hearts the good cheer, the hope, and the faith in the Father's providence, His divine loving grace especially to the meek, the pure of heart, and strong in faith. Oh, my heart overflows and it overflows at this nine or ten in the morning so I scream and I scream in joy even more! My boyfriend laughs as I now talk to the birds, the fairies, and the elves! My heart has not known of this joy, of this happiness, of this bliss! Ah, love's the fairest, more fair than what they call as snow, higher than the clouds, divine more than magical, close, too close to eternity, or is it eternity, itself? My new world continues to bring me all those colors of the rainbow in every single thing I see as Enzo takes me to the ROADS OF GREAT TRUE LOVE!

We stop under a perfect shade. The Acacia is far from foreboding and sullen. In fact, its long huge branches are so graciously welcoming. Enzo takes out the big maroon umbrella. Yes, maroon as ever. That summer solstice happened in UP. That first gust of April wind came in the UP College of Education, Rm. 320. Truthfully, the very first encounter took place in Diliman one day, when the sun was high. 1984.

BACK IN TIME! My white sneakers seemed to be taking the road less taken. I just took my quick lunch of fastfood at the CASAA, behind the old UPD Registrar's Building, and the College of Social Sciences and Philosophy. As usual, I was alone with my books and bright floral notebooks while sipping the rest of my soda with the almost giving up yellow straw [Ma'am Cendana would advise us back in college there's no shame from eating or drinking coffee while walking as every second counts. But of course, I was also wary of getting run over by some speeding blue bus!]. I've always been alone, more like a solitary reaper, but that was before 1992.

Strange but my heart seems listless and restless. I still have one class. My first Academic Semester in my M.Ed.in Educational Administration. My father's choice; he'd always wanted to see me a public school superintendent, the influence of our maternal English speaking grandparents besides the fact that one of my childhood playtimes was to gather everyone, including my older siblings and cousins to teach them of whatever I could manage like how to run fast back home from the fields before the "brown belt" parks in the garage, or how to catch the flying sugarcanes of *Nana* Tibang [!], as well as tell them little crazy and fun stories, or putting them all in a Miss Universe pageant, that we'd then be applying make up on our brother, with him clad in a two-piece bikini then the evening gown of our late mother, or the *ules* merchandize of our *lilang*! The walk back to Benitez Hall feels like the ambivalent feelings of Alfredo in Paz Marquez-Benitez's masterpiece, "Dead Stars," the best short story in English after the American Regime in the country, and how I loved my UST professor in Philippine Literature, Mrs. Gloria Hernandez taught the story to our class, reading the dramatic and climactic lines to us in the most dynamic of phonetics, with her eyes directed and fixed to the ceiling of our room as if she was at the peak of all the most glorious of divine heights! Oh, it seems, today, something is to take place yet I pretend I am not going for it! Then a man. A tall lanky brown man. A Filipino Pierce Brosnan! His denims look typical, in fact, they are shy. His checkered short sleeved-polo feels nice and warm. His hair. So black and thick. Oh, they are in a manly ponytail, no, an eccentric's, an intellectual's, unmistakenly very UP! He is walking ahead of me. I am trailing behind him. Just the two of us; no *tikbalangs* no *kapres* [Philippine supernatural creatures] yet. We're like in some time machine! The world seems different, the pathways look odd. There are gardens and gardens of roses, garlands on his neck, garlands on mine! His strides are princely, gallant but courteous, confident, intelligent, full of wisdom. Then he turns a little and looks at me. He smiles right through my eyes. Time blushes for a second, my heart jumps! The horror and the love tragedy of the old flick involving Count Dracula and his Emily are flashed before me, and tears well in my eyes as the man with the checkered polo disappears in my sight…I am twenty years old. 1984. UNIVERSITY OF THE PHILIPPINES, DILIMAN.

An amiable *maya* alights on the maroon umbrella. Enzo has just cleared the grassy spot with some dry little wood. I help him spread a dainty cloth. Oh, we are obviously on a picnic by the Bustos stream, with the thick *talahib* [willows] bent gracefully, and the vast stretch of the Bulacan town's ricefields. At some distance across, women are merrily washing with their wooden *pamalos* their *batyas* of their household's laundry, and perhaps, of some *donas* [matron]. Several meters away, a big farmhouse in cowboy brick and color sits peacefully with a stable of elegant horses. A caretaker is cleaning." Enzo, we used to have a big chicken house, pigpens, even a great dog! We'd clean the pigpens laughing a lot as our little hands and feet got dirty! Oh, we had goats as well, I think even ducks and rabbits! Ah, we also had turtles and a monkey! At that time, monkeys would just walk down from the mountains, and pay their rent by taking those crawling *kuto at lisa* [vermin and lice] from little girs' heads! Oh, I had them pounding my little brain! Maybe, they were responsible for the mischief in one of my four neurons [Thanks forever Joemar Lazaro Furigay!]. Yeah, *Papang* and

*Mamang* loved all the animals! *Lilang* Andang was so kind with cats that she'd put the kittens and their mom in a box, covering them with her old but clean *ules! Naku,* they were warm and cool in our underground, our basement so that they kept on multiplying, with all the corn, the chikoo [nispero], and the chesa [canistel] of *Lilang*, tucked underneath clean, sun-dried laundry plus her bottles of *Sioktong, boggoong,* and *basi,* not to forget her *baul* of folktales and folklore!" I excitedly share with my boyfriend our family ties and long history with the fauna, fowls included, and of course, the flora. Enzo's face brightens more as he likewise tells me his *Tatang* [father] Berto was popular in their hometown, Meycauayan for being the best and fastest *karitela* or *calesa* driver. He was tagged in his heydays as *Bertong Alimasag* [like a crab man!]. Enzo further tells me and as proudly that he used to take charge of his *Tatang's* stag, take the *calesa* to and fro the public market, and race with other *karitelas* especially at dusk. Maybe the idyllic surroundings, so verdured and golden, are just too inviting and powerful for memories of childhood and family life that the rest of the hours and moments of the lovers' first date are spent on memory lane with every four and two-legged gentle and warm creatures, either as pets or as additional sources of income for the similarly big families [and we didn't know, this served then as a wonderful foreshadowing of our homelife in the bliss of our marriage twelve years later!]. Nonetheless, the two excited very much in love star crossed lovers also recite of their poetry [oh, Frost, Blake, Dickinson, Wordsworth, and Shakespeare, not to forget Jose Garcia Villa, topped our list!], talk of their books [ah, history was superb!], and favorite authors, including their special devotions to saints and the Blessed Mother. Little novena prayerbooks, rosary bracelets, and inspirational readings keep coming from the very new blue Gansport knapsack, including the HOLY BIBLE [which he then gives me with a loving kiss after writing the words of his heart and soul I'd keep to my grave and beyond!], and a cute souvenir of the Statue of Liberty plus Baliwag *chicharon!* The attractive Adonis becomes more and more lovable, mysterious, and interesting; his love for God and his faith in Him are exceptionally admirable, enviable, and inspiring! The lady-beloved soon falls asleep on the broad loving shoulders and firm nice chest of her prince charming, who is no longer just a dream or a fairytale! His *maikling kwentos* [short stories] and *bugtongs* [riddles] send her happily to sound slumber under the cool trees, by the joyful stream, and lovely rice paddies of BULACAN, her beloved's birthplace. From this day on to the next twenty-four years, all the pastries and delicacies of the home province of the Philippines'greatest poet, Francisco Baltazar, more popularly known as Balagtas of the timeless "Florante At Laura," would then come as sweetest surprises, either in early mornings or at midnights, regular days or special occasions from such a most patient, most kind, most romantic loving man named ENZO "ENZO" QUIAMBAO QUIAMBAO, the brilliant, dedicated, dashingly handsome, well-loved and highly respected UP Diliman professor, *"ANG DAKILANG GURO NG MGA ISKOLAR NG BAYAN."*

THERE CAN NEVER BE!

O, Love so true, tender, and young
And Lovers born of eternity's wish, time flutters sweet---
Ah, the bow and the arrow, cast the mystery of destiny's greatest pleasure!
What magic the winds do bring
For the purple blooms of Arabia, and the playful earth of Santa!
THERE CAN NEVER BE!

---ebQuiambao 2019

The next days, weeks, and months from that very first date in Bustos, saw the two lovers of a seventeen-year age difference driving mostly in North Luzon Expressway [NLEX], with rows and rows of the *Agoho*, waving in welcoming delight, and on the wide and fun narrow roads, visiting and introducing me to his family in their old family house in Malhacan, returning often to that first rendezvous of a paradise for more and endless picnics, going around more towns of the province of Bulacan, offering *Sampaguitas*, lighting candles for the dead and the living, of course, our hearts's wishes, and hearing masses in old and new churches and chapels especially the Chapel of the *Tres Personas* [Holy Trinity] in Malolos, the historic Barasoain Church, Guiguinto Church, and all others, eating lunch or early dinner at then top, El Bulakeno in Marilao, home of the superb *crispy pata*, some exotic and *lutong bahay* meals in native or floating restaurants, barbecues in Meycauayan, *meriendas* of the best *lugaw, goto, arroz caldo, bihon, lumpia,* in *turo-turos* along the highways of Guiguinto, of course, never missing the all time favorite, *inipit* at Eurobake, and some *paseo de pasear* along a Red District [as Enzo wrote then a play titled, "Ang Pag-ibig Ni Hudas" [Love's Betrayal!], set in a typical prosti bar or brothel of the town [it's public knowledge!], and staged at the Benitez Hall in UPD] plus a quick tour in the stores of famous firecrackers. All those dates were pages in Cartland's and in every Mills 'N Boon, with Enzo so gentlemanly, so thoughtful, so caring and a hundred per cent, passionate, a real Shakespearean Romeo, a true Lawrence of Arabia, an incomparable Florante of that much celebrated Filipino metrical romance! The town of BALAGTAS keeps the most beautiful secret of the LOVE STORY that began one summer afternoon at the College of Education, University of the Philippines [UP], Diliman, Quezon City.

TWELVE YEARS OF WAITING:Temples of Woe and the English Tagmemic Antidote

Before I met Enzo, April of 1992, I was a high school English teacher. On my last year in the exclusive school for girls that ranked either number one or two at the time and up to this day among all the country's prestigious private schools for girls only, I was in charge of all the seven senior sections of English. I had to teach them World Literature but we lingered on Greek Mythology, my obsession and fascination [Enzo's too!], which sent Dr. Michael Long [renowned linguist, author, Literature Professor then in Cambridge University, Fulbright Visiting Professor, UP] laughing thunderously and shaking his head when I informed him during one of our special summer class sessions in UPD that I was intoxicating my high school students with the Grecian deities in the sprawling perfectly green campus, holding classes by the Calachuchi trees and the bright gardens, all in their choice gods' and demigods' costumes [including the crazy English teacher who'd usually experiment with her haircut!], and that most were in love with the Trojan Prince, Paris except for two who abhorred and cursed him, and sided with King Menelaus, as both girls came from broken families! Of course, the story of Penelope, the faithful and smart wife of Odysseus. I fancied her in as much as I loved Hector's Andromache'[I spent an entire semester with the UE Manila English Majors, teaching that farewell episode of the great Trojan hero to his tearful wife that my infatuated medical student couldn't wait to have me as his girlfriend, oh la la!], and the beautiful Helen of Troy [for the face that launched a thousand nukes, oh, ships [!] but so cursed by clairvoyant, Cassandra, the sister of her lover, Paris. Was destiny making its mean joke then?

WE were so fatally attracted to each other. WE WERE SO IN LOVE! But, our love story was not one usual plot, not the preferred storyline; it had to wait twelve hundred years [beating Gabriel Garcia Marquez's "One Hundred Years of Solitude" but surely, with the grand twist of eximinious magical realism!] before the crescent moon appeared! Ours was written in heaven, maybe by some romantic lyric saint, could be Sara Teasdale if she earned divine pardon[!], or love-struck, prophet [oh no, not King Solomon! Perhaps, the goddess of mischief, Eris sneaked in Paradise!] while Jesus was probably asleep! Hence, professor and student found themselves in the succeeding twelve years learning to cope with the tears, beat the odds, surmount their fears, and wait for that golden moment upon which the blessing of the sacrament of matrimony would so declare [yes, phatic-declarative!] their union to eternity! Enzo continued to teach in UP, wrote more books, undertook a number of research, lectured in seminars, workshops, and conferences while he wrestled with the parodies and exigencies of life. While doing all these, his heart and soul were with me. I then transferred from the Royal Pontifical University after I was scolded by my Dean for absenteeism [oh, the romance, the road trips, and my frail body as I've always been sickly since childhood, our town's two doctors, Dr. Espanto and Dra. Siony De la Cueva would alternately come to the house on a weekly basis! Thank you to the good doctors to the *Barrios!*]to the Benedictine-run SAN BEDA COLLEGE, MENDIOLA, an exclusive school for boys at the time with some of the best NCAA basketball players, and later, PBA players. I stayed there for eight years as a professor of English and Research while serving as the editor-in-chief of the faculty journal of the College of Arts and Sciences, where I had the privilege to edit the works of one of the most brilliant, radically sophisticated Philippine historians, Ambeth Ocampo. I also taught part-time at De La Salle University, Taft. And while busying myself teaching Standard American English [SAE] but of course, always with the native flair and flavour [world Englishes or the Kachruvian paradigm was unheard of yet in the islands at the time [or maybe I was absent in Diliman, swinging by the boughs or aloft my trees of delight!] but my tagmemics, phonetics, and systemic grammar would always subconsciously hail the liberating criteria of intelligibility [making sense though one would sound like my dear twin, the poetess kakapo!], interpretability [oh, the exegete's fancy!], and acceptability [as when you kiss cheek to cheek the enemy with your sporadic English!], as well as the indigenized surface and deep structures with my poetic rebellion in between, oh a streusel of the grammar of radical heresy! Thus, I was almost tossed to burn in hell, at age twenty, by my principal, a stern but witty nun, when I retorted in argumentative register that man does live on bread, if you break down the sentence into its semantic logical units [therefore, he needs SALARY INCREASE!] when she quoted the Holy Bible's "Man does not live on bread alone..." because she was dizzy with her fiscal management, hence, she said, Jesus feeds men with His words! My gay friend, a Music Major in UPD and brother of a hot and sultry singer, couldn't hide his disgust during the debate with the economizing holy veil so he screamed in his nice soprano, "You must be menopausal to forget of your own body, Sr.!" Well, on the following year, the witty sister would then be convincing me to stay with them but I felt I needed to branch out at the time to some other unknown kingdom, at least to my periphery. Three years after, I was fired by my rich lay principal for arguing the semantic truthfulness of critical discourse, when my linguistic parlance put her ineptitude as obvious subject and even its expletive for the prescriptive rule of S-V-O, in the active voice as well as its reverse, the passive, upon Chomsky's Principle of Permutation! Later in the state university, my aristocrat professor changed my final grade from 1.0 [A] to 1.25 [A-] when I asserted the representational langue, poverty is an issue of the intellect more than a harlot of the tongue when she dropped the autocratic unfeeling statement by which mendicity or pauperism, according to her, is an obnoxious, moronic vice, oh!], and how to write the college thesis [whether the traditional or modern but I wanted them to learn how to merge both as text and genre linguistics easily morph [noun to verb?] in the post modern discourse frames, with the trend for intertextuality!] to those naughty but sweet, thoughtful, and loving ambitious Bedans [We'd stay all day long even overnight having those cumbersome but rewarding oral exams with no less than the Benedictine monk, the dean, making a night watch on us! One of them was Jose Sixto, a popular matinee idol [until now!]who patiently waited for his turn to defend his thesis, and which he successfully hurdled; well, Jeremy Marquez too, such sweet young man with a good sense of humor, who'd fret and smoke his cigarette with his classmates whenever their odd English professor was nowhere in the classroom yet and upon her historic arrival before the Red Lions's kingdom [by the entrance gate], every naughty Bedan, and those very tall NCAA players [my *barkada* then at breaktime eating my favorite, *goto!* They'd teach me how to spice it more 'til my tongue burned!] would be squatting by the driveway! But they'd soon be driving her sedan to the back parking lot to give their crazy late professor [oh, that bad insomnia as ever, and the many times I got lost with my red Hyundai in some alley, trying to avoid the terrible traffic!] time to run to the ladies room [Oh, how often would I chance then on Madam with the sophisticated scarf!], powder herself, and fix her stubborn dry hair as the boys would usually ask her, "Ma'am, *mahangin ba sa labas?*" Racing cars of Bedans would frequent my Blue Ridge or Kalayaan units at late nights for they knew their professor was a notorious owl [!], with the boys bringing [or bribing?] me midnight snacks while they'd consult their thesis or some perplexing English grammar or syntax [oh, how direct translation from L1 to L2 or vice versa would make us all laughing 'til dawn!]. Yes, grammar by midnight, I'd be persistently tempted to teach the boys more of descriptive grammar in the moonlight as in not losing the cadence of linguistic intimacy [Martin Joos's Degrees of Language Formality] as they'd fiercely climb the corporate ladder [with their good business English and some foreign tongue like the nice French, German, Spanish, Nihonggo, or Fookien!] to the CEO's office, play their golf, jetset over continents because one day, they might just come home with all the *kale*, the carpet and the furnishings but no queen to keep a man's sanity in check, while the prescriptive systemics via an eclectic communicative approach [CLTA!] by day time as in which syntactic construction dynamics would persist in ultramodern thought, which word classes to promote *harmonia* or *concordia* in the face of critical, academic or intellectual, even cultural upheavals, belligerence, or bigotry, which lexical heritage to dominate in the economic, political, and territorial or sovereign claims or disputes, which morphological unit to create or re-create, bind or unbind new forms of religious, ethical and civilized interactions, which rules of grammar to extenuate issues of ignorance, mediocrity, superficiality while such syntagmatics with also the corresponding paradigmatics blast the walls of oppression, social injustice, apathy and enmity, hostilities, acts of terrorism and all forms or variants of violence! Well, the idealistic English teacher in me, more of my favorite Linda Carter's classic, Wonderwoman, or the *Pinoy, Darna*!]] as well as to the more serious, quite driven La Sallians [with everyone looking at their watches whenever I was late! One, the cutest boy, seemed to have become infatuated with his peculiar professor after she lectured on the philosophy of love [Well, I just had published then in UP Education Quarterly for my essays on love!] as rationale or framework for critiquing the ethics of cloning [but in Loyola, I gave them cryogenics while in Espana, I taught them cryptology!] in their writing class that he'd hide behind the door until everyone had left for him to walk her to the gates, Jesus!], I was also finishing my doctoral studies in UPD, with me occasionally dropping all my books as I'd climb the jampacked "Katas Ng Saudi," trying to reconcile dogma and non-absolutism[!]in my feeble brain, with my overly eccentric professor in Educational Philosophy telling me to brace myself for our partnership in founding a truly egalitarian university in the Mountain province [!] in between her erudite bites of the chicken empanada I'd bring for her [oh, as I'd disappear from time to time in her class with two of my naughty more senior classmates, one a smart Protestant part-time faculty, and who'd pamper her boss with all the *kaldero* and the plastic dining set of a not so-environmental friendly constellation!], and stepping on some toes in the speeding reckless jeepney of the loudest colors and stereo, at one time, a mischievous old man touched my butt [maybe he liked my Spanish flowing skirt!], I couldn't slap him with the libraries in my hand and my high respect for the elderly! However, one time, I had to walk and pretend I was the lost Sophia Loren of the movie, "Sunflower" because the nasty strong winds blew so hard my long *senorita skirt,* my half body [oh, just too glad the other half doesn't fly at night nor levitate!] was exposed unannounced before the overflowing population of Gastambide, and the tricycle drivers whistled, clapped their shameless hands, and cried their gratitude to the conspiring winds! Of course, I got those legs and cute butt from my Spanish Mama! At one time, while lecturing a la Sermon on the Mount on the pragmatic philosophy of stylistics and mechanics in writing the expository cum literary essay before my senior Philosophy majors English class, everyone couldn't seem to look at me, with heads bowed down as if karats of gold were all scattered on the floor except for one naughty head and pair of curious eyes. But the saint among those young men just couldn't bear it anymore thus he came up bashfully to me and whispered, "Ma'am, your zipper is open!" Good God, my dainty pink Karimadon slacks was suddenly a huge shame for me[I couldn't even recall if my underwear was pink also, in my shock!], that three of my nicest students had to surround me like scout rangers as I made my *pas de bouree* to the comfort room! But we had to walk past two law classrooms, and that time, they were on a break, with most of the law students on the corridors, and how the four of us pretended we were in some *pas de quatre*! Then, one indiscreet but well, mega admiring [thank you!] bar hopeful commented, "Ph.D. from UP pala ang P.I.!]What a nice compliment from a budding lawyer! Oh, my zipper henceforth became my discourse topic in Loyola as I exemplified what subjects would make good memoirs. Another embarrassing episode upon which my sweet protective Bedans would make the *pas de trois* with their goofy English professor was when she had stained her cream slacks this time with her monthly period getting so profusely vigorous and oh, upsetting! The young men were just as understanding and cool like how they composed themselves when their Theology professor just couldn't stop her menstruation from trickling down to the platform, with her wearing a pretty floral dress! AHHHHH WOMEN!!! I gradually moved completely to Ateneo de Manila University upon my Ph.D. graduation in 2000, giving up with a heavy heart my Bedan family, my editorship, the Professorial Chair awarded to me by the SBC Alumni Association, and of course, my security of tenure! In all those years, my heart and soul were with Professor Enzo Q. Quiambao, my boyfriend, my lover, my beloved! Those twelve years of long engagement saw us struggle with ourselves, with the difficulties of *pas de deux,* with our own vulnerabilities, including the grump of destiny. We'd bear with our respective temples of woe while ESL and EFL buoyed our positive energies to philanthropic and patriotic sense of nation! We just kept on doing what we needed to do and what we longed to do to live our lives in the sun and to glorify our God despite all the hardships, the sacrifices, the pains, and well, the folly. TWELVE YEARS. They did not come easy. They were never perfect. But we were happy. Then, the long wait was over. The best ever iridescent rainbow ascended to the skies for Enzo to now marry me. This was in 2005.

But before the papers came, there were tempests to weather, raging waves to survive, battles to win. Right at the beginning.

DANGEROUS LIASONS. TEMPTATIONS. It was supposedly our first month anniversary as sweethearts. It should have been perfectly fun, joyful, and grateful. Unfortunately, like in any other love story, in every fairytale, AN UGLY WITCH [oh, she was real sizzling hot!] with an Apple of Poison! But well, not exactly the case but the Yellow Monster!

She walked past me from the College of Education [COE] entrance. She was wearing the shortest skimpiest shorts in the campus. Her tube blouse was almost falling except that she was clearly more than blessed. Her breasts were like our homegrown *papayas*; big, full, large but they looked not as firm and proud as the Mayon's perfect glory. Her face and skin bore the sophistication and class of the affluent. Her name? Never mind! Oh, I adore you to the stars, William S.!

I tried to overtake her with my Marikina shoes but she darted a la Lydia De Vega to Rm. 107 and locked the door! Jesus Christ! I kept knocking but obviously, nobody heard me, not even my boyfriend who was inside that room! I was silently furious but there was nothing much I could do but sit and wait on those benches outside Rm. 107. Thirty minutes of damning eternity or so passed. The door opened. The voluptuous woman came out with a dishevelled curly hair, sweat on her forehead, her perspiration trickling down her equally dishevelled tube, her shorts more now like a bikini worn in haste! The undergrad students covered their mouths as the male eyes popped! I stormed inside Rm. 107 like a fully loaded whissing misdirected missile!

Enzo was seated as usual behind his table, writing, with his reading glasses. His hair looked very neat and gorgeous as usual. His clothes were as decent as usual. But there were just too many books piled up on the right side of his table. My imported RAYBAN sunglasses flew! My bag with my surprise little gift of a local Jovan and anniversary card sealed with a kiss flew! My chocolate brown sandals also flew! The target? My boyfriend! Then I cried, no, I screamed and cursed, and charged like the wild wild west, oh, wild wild mare of the most ferocious most notorious boondocks! My fingernails dug into his thick hair, and they pulled the black and gray! Oh man, the professor of Diliman certainly knew he was doomed and he was damned, so he tried to run and avoid the next cannon ball! But I've always been an Indian war girl at my playtime especially when I sensed the enemy, so I lifted one book after the other and hit the target bull's eye, one after the other! I was Rizal's *Sisa*, I was my great great grandmother's [Gabriela Silang] reincarnate, I was totally the embodiment of the words, "Hell hath seen no fury than a woman scorned!" *Manang Biday* of Ilocandia was perfectly herself! Then Enzo cried. He cried! He picked up one by one my mess. He started with my very expensive sunglasses, his gift to me. Oh, they were broken! Next, he picked up my bag, my lipstick, my baby powder, my cologne, and my pink comb, then the still wrapped surprise little gift and the card with the kiss. Oh, at least they were fine, with maybe, the kiss still fresh! Then he picked up my pair of Marikina *sandals*. Oh, they were heavy! My heart was in pieces, and I was dead guilty for my bandit, my brusqueness, and my MORTAL SIN! I accused my boyfriend with my rash, unfounded conclusion! I didn't even give him a chance to open his mouth and explain who really was that hot vixen, why the door got locked, and why he couldn't hear my knocking then as well as why the pile of books on the right side of his table! I just went berserk with anger and gotten blinded with jealousy! Indeed, I was jaundiced with crazy jealousy! My judgment was totally impaired that my excessive jealousy made me see the horrible ghost of my incredibly devastating insecurity! My physics, geometry, and calculus were too faulty again! I thought velocity impacted quadruple to upward trajectory on height and space then skewed to a narra table! So I sat down on the chair of Professor Madamba, hoping his genius in Math would help me extrapolate on the factors of time, tension, and sweat. Enzo shared the room with him and Dr. Omila, my excellent Statistics professor. Fortunately that time they had classes. Enzo picked up his books as he was explaining but his tears just kept flowing, and he was crying out for help to his dead *Tatang Berto [father]* and to his dead *Inang Norayda [mother]*. My heart couldn't bear it anymore! I ran to him, actually, jumped on him, and hugged him so tight and kissed him all over his face, his hair, his hands, oh, his hands! We kissed and made up in no time as we then drove to Bustos, our paradise [!], where we made love a la Michael Douglas and Sharon Stone in their flicks, by the jealous stream, the conspiring willows, and the chirping fowls, so tickled in their nests! The poetry of husband and wife, Robert and Elizabeth Browning complemented to the heavens the fire of love's 'aflaming' as we were drunk with the overflowing honey of passion, each one with a word, a verse, and lots of onomatopoeia [!],[of course, as one book I read in college said, love is a lot more exciting as lovers get noisier! Just be accurate with the name but no worries with homophones! And make sure to spell each letter with stylistic phonemics if partner is obsessive-compulsive with orthography!], to exclaim and exalt the incomparable ecstasy and joy of subliminal perfection! Gee, that also, could have been some scene in Cartland's as her characters were caught in crimes of passion! Oh, not really the psychological thriller of Douglas and Glenn Close's "Fatal Attraction" though almost like it, I suppose! From then on, after every big fight, that dainty cloth was ever present and ready for the passionate lovers' honeymooning, either in that paradise by the willows and stream or by the open fields [when it drizzled and whenever King Sun beamed!], or in some university campus [oh, how passion could make mad lovers out of the bored be-spectacled beings!], when dusk had set in, under those huge Acacia trees, with the two adult- maroons romantically hiding from the eyes of the patrolling police! One odd time, love's consummation just couldn't wait that the dainty cloth was spread under a majestic though melancholic huge *balite* [Ficus], near some ancient cemetery as we have just visited and prayed for the dead, with my boyfriend reciting his most sentimental *tula* and so I felt I needed to complement it with a line or two, hence, "A Riddle or the Cricket's Cry Is to Doubt a fit Reply!"[Blake's "Auguries of Innocence"]! At this point, my boyfriend unleashed all the possible riddles in the world that we soon rolled on the damp ground in laughter, sending the big *uwak* [crow] looking for some other nest! How odd we really were but the cemetery of an ancient world seemed to understand that the lovers might have been as passionate lovers also in a much earlier world in a thousand of years! Love and romance, romance and love have never made life dull and unexciting but bursting and pulsating even in the skeletons of time! All the passionate trysts would then culminate with the lovers' visits to chapels and churches for the guilt in their souls, the dogma in their heads, and the ethics of their profession! Of course, lovers' delightful and honeymooning years are never without the cup of sin! Romantic love is both the nest of incomparable happiness but can also be the tempting gin for the soul as passion in love is no invincibility of human beings that is why the surrealism, impressionism, and oh, naturalism in the typography of paintings and sculpture plus the prosopography of poets, fictionists, and of biographers and memoirists! And who could ever forget the perfect romance and biting realism of my other Hollywood favorite, Meryll Streep's "Bridges Of Madison County"? My God, I think I was in freshman college when I saw the flick and how I envied Meryll as she stood in amazing nudeness by the door of her small home as the eyes of her secret lover hiding in the dark were on her womanly perfection while the wind engulfed the woman to another spiritus mundi! That movie is one hellish of superior art and obra-romantic yet real, real yet surreal, it lifts you to unknown heights then it kicks your butt to pick the pieces of one's mess then move on with real world! How about the classics "Gone With The Wind," Emily Bronte's "Wuthering Heights," Nathaniel Hawthorne's "The Scarlet Letter," and oh, D.H. Lawrence's "Lady Chatterley's Lover" that my foolish class lectures in Loyola would seem to get my graduate student, Erick Salud, a television and film director cogitating and thinking aloud of his next romantic obra, and the young Korean beauty smiling that one day she would then become the girlfriend of the bachelor President at the time! But, being devout Catholics, Enzo and I knew we needed to earn back heaven's favors and blessings despite and in spite of our obsequious and preposterous rationalizations and justifications to grave culpability. In no time, we then rode the jampacked train to Baclaran Church where we bought in its side streets the best crabs ever, that which when dipped in Ilocos *suka* [sugarcane vinegar] with most spicy *sili* [pepper], you'd forget your name! But of course, we also took the notorious colourful speeding jeepney to Quiapo Church after which we proceeded to the altar on bended knees but humans indeed need food to nourish the body whereupon the next itinerary would be Ongpin or China town to gorge and bloat on the best of exotic oriental cuisine, and we literally joined the Holy Week's uphill life- and- death walk of penitence to Antipolo Church that I literally swallowed about three *balot* out of extreme exhaustion and hunger as we reached the church! I'd then ask a priest in the confessionary box if sex was evil! His answer? "Are you a prostitute?" Good God [!], I left in haste without knowing my penance! I then comforted myself with grilled jumbo hotdog for supper, allowed the cockroach to live, and read the Book of Revelation! I also prayed for the priest not to scare those in the flesh trade and all other sinful mortals from confessing their sins, so as to move the population statistic towards heaven, and perforate hell! Well, I likewise wished for the holy father to see Richard Gere and Julia Roberts' "Pretty Woman." And I'm sure, today, heaven is getting more immigrants from the two much much lower worlds [purgatory and hell] as Pope Francis becomes more adept and versatile with his holy twit! But well, maybe, a number are LOST IN EREBUS as temptations are a lot more deliciously, desirously, instantly compelling and inviting so perhaps they need to read my book, LOST IN EREBUS...THE LONGEST PRAYER. Hopefully, more immigrants to heaven afterwards, and no more skewing the normal curve to Luci's kingdom!

They took me home past midnight. It was February 15, 1997. My *barkada*, my colleagues in San Beda just dropped me off in my Blue Ridge studio apartment which had a nice terrace that Enzo and I would decorate with Christmas lights and a big *parol* in December as well as ornamental hanging plants *luha ng dalaga* [Enzo then won't agree to the plant but my artistic insolence prevailed over the superstition!], cute variety of cactus, and bubbly roses all the way from Guiguinto, Bulacan. I didn't know my boyfriend was long waiting for me, clad in my gift of *avocado*-green Collezione jacket, so he looked like a policeman or the famous sleuth, Sherlock Holmes in his brand new owner stainless jeep, Sylvester Stallone. But of course, I asked much earlier his permission if I could join the evening group eat out in Greenhills, February 14. Since we'd celebrate our Valentine's on the following weekend in picturesque Antipolo as he had late night classes and he'd given me my sweet bouquet of roses and almond chocolates with the thoughtful singing cards early morning, I thought it would be okay to spend some time with my good friends [five boys, two girls plus myself]. Besides, I'd usually turn them down in most of our group dinners especially when these occasions were in high-end business district, Makati as Enzo would not allow me to go that far and come home late without him to accompany me. Oh, the moment my friends' cars left, Enzo followed me from where he was secretly hiding, and seriously dealt with me until we got inside my studio. He was angry and he was teary eyed. He had so many questions. I could not even pee from my surprise, and oh, my guilt! Not that I was fooling around but I had a great time with my friends since they let me sing with a nice microphone in an exclusive videoke bar, and my grade was 75! I sang "Love me tender love me sweet, oh my dreams complete!", my favorite childhood song that my father and older siblings would even then record, not so much for the voice but for the memory [with me sticking that charcoal- roasted hotdog in my mouth!] and the sentiment [dramatic singing face with the accompanying segmentals and supra-segmentals, multimodality complete[!], at about nine or ten years old!]; oh, how I loved Pilita Corrales especially when she'd bend sexy and classy as she sang *Dahil Sa Iyo,* and the soprano Armida Siguion-Reyna with the interesting tongue! I was also wearing that Valentine's night a new *corduroy*-like red blouse, dear Lord [!], with the curious eyes of other tired and enjoying yuppies [doctors of medicine, oh!] on me. In fact, I just drove for the very first time my brand new second hand red Hyundai four-door sedan, courtesy of my older sister, Erleen and her lawyer-husband, *Manong* Boy [I paid them five thousand pesos monthly for the next five years!]. My will power and my being a risk-taker fuelled my confidence to drive [after a three-day driving school in A-1!] all the way from the garage of my sister's house in Village East, Cainta to Blueridge then to Greenhills with my friend, former seminarian, Albert who seemed not to be breathing while I drove like we were in a bump car in Fiesta Carnival, and tires screeching no end, other motorists thought we were ready for a drag race! We then got stuck on a curve going up Aurora Boulevard from Marcos Highway as I forgot to switch gears from *tercera to primera,* with a jesting nun stopping for a second on her L300, lowered her window to laugh on me and my profusely sweating good friend, and how we cursed that incredible holy veil out of sheer fatigue and exasperation but which would then become such a funny memory for the two old pals! Oh, my boyfriend just could not help but worry then so he waited and waited for his overly maverick, at times funky yet old-fashioned girlfriend to drive back safely home, with her bones and soul in tact. But, our friend, Inday, a terrific and crazy *collegiala* Math professor, did the driving back to my place with her fettish *bumalabs* [awful mistake!] expression, together with our pretty *kayumanggi Pangalatok* so toughy lawyer friend, Lani seated at the back, with her taxation and canon laws, sharing to us her hilarious blind dates [oh men, how could you be all so amusingly ridiculous and real fools at times!] while our male friends rode with their bills, receipts, and credit cards in the other cars. Enzo was not like me [ferocious and dangerous!] though whenever he got jealous; he'd just wait, write me *hugot* [sentimental] notes, leave *Rodic's* food and *inipit* [oh, killing me softly with kindness!]on the table, then listen quietly and patiently with his swelling tears to my confessions or alibis or explanations. Of course I was much younger than him and there were moments I wanted to have some little fun with my trusted friends when days and nights were just too lonely as he couldn't be with me [oh, we did not live in!] or visit me all the time. His work, and the cares of the world would take him away for several days or sometimes two weeks from me. Oh well, I was really one spoiled girlfriend, so demanding, so doubtful and doubting, insecure and all the more as time made its cruising to eternity! Twelve years of that life really put my patience, my fidelity, my sanity to the edges but it seemed I was even more than Grecian Penelope for I never let anyone come too dangerously close while my Odysseus was in some voyage in a far away land. Oh, except for one.

He was a landscape architect, twelve years my junior. A very cute guy with big smart eyes and quite huge head; a typical brainy. Our students started pairing us up. Weird as I was not a bit interested [at the beginning?!] and more than annoyed! I was much older and even taller! But he seemed to like my jokes, stories, and teaching *antics* a lot [from my naughty students'anecdotes of me to him, like saying good-bye to the next class when I've just entered the room, or asking them just one question in their midterms, on why the sun keeps on shining! Or, designing English exams only gay Bedans would pass that when their famous classmate hurdled it with just five others making it as well, of course, all so gay and smart, everyone cheered and jeered out of sheer amazement and pleasant laughter!], even my extreme temperaments! One time that our yuppies group went for our pre- Christmas celebration somewhere in culture-rich Malate, with all the legitimate and budding artists [their books, paintings, and sculpture everywhere!] drinking, singing, and having a good time, he kept moving close to me at the back seat of my car that I was ready to slap him if he moved even much closer! Thank God, he sensed I was ill at ease [though I liked his masculine perfume and his rather big ears as I've always been fascinated with elves!], and he quit moving like a penalized young corporal! We then went walking like happy nomads, forgetting our piles of testpapers and grades'deadlines by the breakwater area in Manila Bay and Luneta or Rizal Park, of course with no controversial photobomber yet to spoil the fun. Next time around, I caught the guy looking at me with those nice eyes, a sweet amused smile on his lips as he sat quietly in a corner of our friend's Sampaloc all *narra* family house while I was bantering in my orange jersey blouse with the rest of our highly spirited *barkada*, and oh, I seemed to develop a crush, a fascination for him like he were some shy but real clever gallant prince, in the days and weeks that followed! But of course, my heart knew where it perched! He tried to woo me by his thoughtful gestures though he was still then in a shaky relationship that would eventually come to an end as the girl wanted another guy, perhaps sensing her boyfriend seemed thinking of someone else. To an extent, I began to like him more especially when he'd listen to my heartaches as I told him of my long-time relationship with Enzo. He was just listening all the time; no judgment, no contempt, no bad vibes. Actually, he seemed to like me more, I presumed as he'd accompany me apply in another prestigious university, with him patiently reading his books [He was also studying philosophy at the time!]on the staircase all day long, cheering me up as there were so many applicants, and henceforth, I gave my demonstration teaching, adopting a socio-historic-political framework in my instant editorial lesson on the heroism of former Philippine President Manuel Roxas, and oh, the panel liked it! He'd also drive me here and there when my boyfriend was too busy in Diliman, Sumulong, and Meycauayan, and could not make it. He'd also tell me of his heartches, his fears, and his dreams. Oh, the naïve flirtation and mutual attraction would then become more and more dangerously appealing to both our quite unstable worlds, with us spending a lot of time together just talking and talking of every possible subject while driving, walking in the entire Ateneo campus, haggling with the *tinderos at tinderas* in buying *bangus at tahong*, making sure there's no Red Tide[!], or simply seated on equally excited corners! I even introduced him to my boyfriend, and a very intelligent man, Enzo seemed to know what to do and how to handle my obvious crush for my friend [the eldest son of a former governor with the Latin honors on his college graduation and a *topnotcher* Board Exam results] who, also, was obviously very much attracted to me [Well, I've always believed I was beautiful in my own unique ugliness, huh!]. Enzo cooked *binating kinamatisang itlog* with a lot of onions [sautéed eggs with tomatoes] for him, for the three of us in his home in UP, and they found out, they were some distant relatives, Jesus! Enzo even volunteered for us to bring my male friend back to his boarding house near the famous historic and miraculous Quiapo Church, well, with all the prying and waiting pickpockets, snatchers, and holduppers [as everyone knows!] around the vicinity of the ever busy historic place plus all kinds of herbs, Betamax tapes, and Chinese ham in every nook and cranny surrounding the revered and beautiful Philippine church with millions of fanatic devotees to the *Santo Kristo, Apo Lakay, Poong Nazareno,* that one of my innocent but smart Atenean English-speaking little nephews would then candidly call as a sacred or holy African! My friend was very much impressed by the kindness of my boyfriend though just like Enzo, he was also an intelligent guy, indeed. He'd talk me out of breaking up with my boyfriend, reminding me of the value of time and the weight of social mores plus heaven, purgatory, and hell! All the more that I got confused with love and religion! I'd then spend so much time at night trying to decipher how passionate romantic love could earn a cool spot in heaven, with God waiving sweet fornication and all others! How my theology would crash on my philosophy and vice versa but what a relief to find poetry in between! Both men would thus do their best to keep the flames burning, each with his own bible verses to quote, brand of philosophy to exhort, plus jokes to make me bloat [!], but of course, destiny prevailed, and my friend and I had to go separate ways after that one night, in a restaurant along E. Rodriguez, he seemed very ready to give me his ring that he obviously was keeping in his pocket but he could not get me promise to break up with my long-time boyfriend! So, we said good-bye to each other, his eyes those of Jack in the timeless, "Titanic" while I planted my quick farewell kiss on his gentlemanly cheek! Our prayers [Enzo's and mine!] to the Blessed Mother [to Our Lady of Antipolo with the longest holy curly hair, and the miraculous tale, to Our Lady of Fatima, very special to my heart as well as Our Lady of Lourdes, and to Our Mother of Perpetual Help, Enzo's special devotion] for her intercessions for our hearts' desires, petitions, and pleadings helped us a lot to withstand the test of time until April 19, 2005 and May 16, 2005.

## TWO WEDDINGS:One With The Judge, The Other With The Jesuit

"Yes, I do!" I was just too overjoyed that I almost yelled my "I do's" to the fabulous judge, wearing an all too amused smile on her lovely well-made up face. Judge Teresa Yadao officiated my civil wedding with my long-time boyfriend of twelve years, some thirty minutes before lunch on 19 April 2005. I was wearing an old pink dainty blouse with more ruffles for my flat chest [That was why growing up, my older brother would always put me in a brawl with him for he must have thought, I was also a boy!], my hair braided to the shoulders, and oh, faded denim pants plus my school black shoes! But to make the occasion more formal, I bought a fuchsia shawl to accentuate the sweet conservative femininity of my blouse, and well, my being, no matter how liberal or radical or odd my thoughts could get at certain times especially when the moon is just too large and low! My elegant though quite loquacious, very fair *Auntie* Purita Tejada, and my younger more than witty sister, Estela Marie were with us to grace and witness the very special day of my life and my Enzo's. My groom was wearing his old green polo *barong* with finely embroidered designs, paired with decent cream pants. His moccasin glistened with the sunlight and the fluorescent. Well, his hair was perfect, and his heart was just as overjoyed as mine; he also said his "I do's!" in such full volume and pitch! The judge laughed all too pleasantly and quite tickled, so did my pretty *kayumanggi* and *balingkinitan* [slender]*tsinita* [chinky-eyed]sister, and our beautiful petite aunt whose husband, the very tall, very big, former U.S. Navy, Uncle Resty with the heavy drool, was at the time working in ARAMCO, Saudi Arabia when the oil was as much, with not too many oil explorations yet in other regions and seas of the planet. Oh, it seemed only a second passed and our civil wedding was over! It took us twelve long gruelling years to be married in just a second of time. Wow! What a masterpiece of destiny! And to add to the dramatic irony, our camera could just take two shots, Jesus Christ! Nonetheless, that beautiful sunny day, with a new Pope [Pope Benedict!] declared a few minutes later our "I do's," was capped with a festive late lunch at Trellis, one of our favorite middle class *Pinoy* restaurants in Quezon City. Together with our aunt's friend, and of course, Estela Marie who could not keep her happiness for her older sister, the newly-married couple enjoyed sizzling pork *sisig, kare-kare* with the good *puso ng saging,* nice *bagoong alamang, inihaw na panga ng tuna, pancit canton,* and pork spare ribs with green mango juice to wash the cholesterol. Dessert came later with nice scoops of *durian* and *ube* ice cream from nearby UP Diliman. Oh, the moment of realization that I was finally married to the man of my dreams after the long wait just made me burp quite loud, sending the little company laughing in joyful mirth. That was my first wedding. With the beautiful vixen of a judge, and my happy big burp!

## My Second Wedding: WITH THE JESUIT

"This is the latest wedding I've ever officiated!" Fr. Manuel "Manny" Flores, SJ exclaims on the pulpit, with an obvious scowl on his cute face. Tonight is the 16th of May 2005, my church wedding at the Holy Trinity [Thank you, *Tres Personas!,* Malolos!] Parish Church, Village East, Cainta, Rizal. The Jesuit priest looks even more handsome than ever especially with the new hair cut. He is the Director of the ARRUPE, the International Jesuit Formation in the Philippines. My young Jesuit seminarian-students in my English, Poetry and Fiction classes in Ateneo de Manila introduced him to me in one of their Wednesday Open Houses. Since then, Fr. Manny and I became very close to each other; he was the perfect Jesuit, while I was the notorious late comer!

"Oh, how much is one small wine glass, and how about that bigger glass over there?" I ask the charming very *Pinay* saleslady. She finally wraps too carefully each one of three dozens of cute wine glasses, and each one as well of another three dozens of the bigger wine glasses, this time with even more careful movements. It takes her almost two hours wrapping my church wedding's souvenir items for the guests and sponsors. Today. Tonight, May 16. It's almost five o' clock in the afternoon. I should be in church by six. Oh, but my wedding car needs carwash! My now nine year-old red Hyundai sedan, my Red Bull, obviously needs shampooing and the tire black, so I drive fast to Maginhawa Street for my car's quick makeover. Ah, there are two more ahead of her. It's 5:30 p.m. I wait with the dusk falling on my fatigue and stress. My phone rings. *Auntie* Purita is adamant for my make up. I thought she earlier said "Ricky Reyes" but we are now inside "Reyes Haircutters" along Anonas. *"Ang sarap niyang make up-an. Ang kinis!* Flawless!" The gay make up artist comments on my *Auntie* who now looks every inch an alluring *diva*, a gorgeous fabulous talkative beautiful little woman. He is working on my blush on. I am tempted to kick him with my pissed off sneakers right there at the center of his universe but I change my mind as he isn't done yet with my eyebrows [Oh, sorry for my little crime in thought! More of the tension of the momentous event! Bridezillah moments!]]. It's past six p.m. I drive back my aunt to their house in Project 2 so she could change into her elegant old rose gown. Old Rose, that's the motif of my church wedding. My very refined, well-mannered dearest, the late uncle Roland [ever so patient with my impulsive ways!] tells me to just drop the first lexeme, hence, only ROSE. I drive like crazy to our Madasalin apartment. Everyone is *gaga* with their lipstick, their foundation, their eyelashes, their manicure, their gowns, their stilettoes, their waistline, their hips, their boobs, their breath! They forget me, the BRIDE. Just like how we forgot then *Manang* Baby Lou in that supposedly *despedida* family picture-taking at the airport before she boarded that plane to Tripoli, with everyone flashing their biggest smiles and no *Manang* Baby Lou in the group! I climb to our bedroom and change from my soiled and sweaty casual wear to my bridal dress. DRESS. Yes, just a dress. Knee-high. In white, of course. There's no time to take another bath so I just pour the purple baby cologne on my body. Oh, my fingers itch, my legs itch, my nape itches so do my ears! I am allergic to any perfume and cologne! I wear the simple white dress I paid for over a thousand pesos to the promising *Mabilbila barrio* seamstress. Yes, I keep the purse now! Oh, she sewed me a nice lace tuft, a shy veil, and a long flowing dreamy bridal lace train. I put on each one but then I forget my cool dainty train as my undies [oh, singular!] makes me feel itchy too! I also poured the purple cologne on my white laced wedding dainty with the cute flirtatious ribbons on the left and on the right plus a more bushy one at the middle! My stepmother knocks on my door to tell me they are now going ahead to the church. Oh, she's divine! She's wearing an interestingly fashionable gown! My *tita* Chelie looks so elegant and beautiful and poised to the max with her little dinner bag! Her footwear is very expensive and formidable as they are quite pointed like the ladies of James Bond! Oh, everyone seems gone as the apartment is suddenly quiet. I quickly pull up the bridal garter to my right thigh, then my beige sequined stilettoes on my frantic excited feet, and rush carelessly downstairs to check if Marvin, my engineer *conyo* [elite] cousin, is ready to bring me to church. He's the hero of my wedding day, oh, wedding night. He's wearing maroon long sleeves, of course as he's a graduate as well of UPD but schooled in Ateneo de Manila for his basic education. His father, Uncle Boy is the most reserved of all my *titos* but very brilliant, efficiently sophisticated, and American educated. Marvin smiles politely at his bride cousin. Andrew, our other very tall and as handsome cousin, a law student at UST, and his girlfriend are just finished with Red Bull, content with the nice orange flowers as they could not find the old rose in Dangwa, where all of Earth's blossoms are sold at much cheaper prices. All set then to go except that I'm already very hungry so I run to the kitchen and stuff my mouth with the Ligo Sardines left over and a cold *pan de sal*. Marvin gently reminds me of the time though he seems to be very nervous as his cute fair *makinis* face looks a little red. It's past 7:30 P.M. I am one hour and more than thirty minutes late to my church wedding! And I am still in Teacher's Village, Quezon City! Village East, Cainta is almost a two hour-drive from Madasalin Street when it's traffic. And it turns out, HEAVY TRAFFIC! Hence, Marvin, the well-bred engineer turns Marvin, the Mad Driver! We arrive at the Holy Trinity Parish Church at 8:30 P.M. with the secondary and principal sponsors, some in their fabulous gowns[!],[Dr. Marlu Vilches, the now ADMU Vice President for Academic Affairs is one of them and Shayne, wife of the Magsaysay and National Artist, Dr. Bien Lumbera!] all perspiring, sweaty, and hungry, including all the guests except my handsome groom! As my elated proud father, *muy* guapo in his delicate beige *Barong,* and beautiful *Tita* Chelie walk me to the Holy Altar [with my father scolding me in a low voice for my tardiness!], adorned with lovely immaculate white blossoms, Enzo looks very dashing on that holy ground in his *pina Barong Tagalog,* my wedding gift to my groom- husband which I bought for over five thousand pesos at the Sy empire! His face is most relieved and very radiant, seeing his bride-wife, in the loving thoughtful pearls of their dear friends, Alex and Detdet Puente [who, at this time are already in Boston with their lovable son, Francis, and Alex enrolled in the Ph.D. English Program at Boston College, of course, with Alex sharing with me so generously kind many of his books like our other friend, John Labella, leaving to me the fine literature of the world as gift before he flew to Princeton, plus his scolding me for being computer illiterate then that Danton Remoto would worry how I could stay long in Loyola when I couldn't even encode my own grades [!], and Charlie Veric, who'd be so kind to encode those grades, with *Ninang* Lulu Reyes reminding him to be patient with me [!], gifting and dedicating to me his poem titled, "Nariyan Ka" [Ever Present] as he prepares then for Yale while I gave him a cute monkey stuff toy for lucky charm but first teaching him how to eat Ilocano *boggoong* with fresh tomatoes, *kamayan* style! Well, Charlie would really remind me to be more cultured with his weekend French, etc. cultural films while he'd accompany me [with his pleasant guffaws!]rent DVD's for *"Ang Pulis At Ang Kembot"* that I'd watch twice to kill the mocking bird of my ennui at midnights!] finally walking down the brilliant red aisle, after twelve years, two hours and thirty minutes! Fr. Manny then castigates me during his homily while the choir, twelve young goodlooking Jesuit seminarians from twelve different countries[China, Japan, Hong Kong, Indonesia, Malaysia, Myanmar, Nepal, Pakistan, Singapore, Taiwan, Thailand, and Vietnam] whisper and chuckle with one another as the Jesuit priest says, "This is the latest wedding of the century!," and looks at me sheepishly. I attempt to stick out my tongue on the good handsome priest but my groom tells me to behave, and he fixes my veil so it won't show the bride's reddish mischievous tongue, oh, so the veil won't fall in no time! Then, the "I do's" and the rings! At this point, heaven seems to have opened its doors, with all the cherubs singing gloriously, together with the choir of the most amazing Jesuit seminarians, loving family, rejoicing friends, relatives, guests, humanity. I felt like farting due to my extreme happiness thus, my Church Wedding before God and before Ateneo de Manila [!], oh, before men, ended with my best air of euphoria with the Jesuit priest now smiling ear to ear as he has just married the vagabond notorious woman [having gone to teach English and Literature to almost all of Metro Manila's top schools, colleges, and universities, UAAP and NCAA [!] to a saint! St. Ignatius of Loyola must be so proud of the Jesuit priest! Maybe, St. Thomas is as happy for the former Thomasian who just cannot hold her subtleties at the apex of excitement! The wedding reception follows with poetry, hymns, songs [with beautiful *kayumanggi Auntie* Sally Tejada singing acapella "The Impossible Dream!"], dedications, buffet, laughter, joy, and TEARS…

LOSING HER! My Rare Wild Blue Orchid

"Mili, how do I look?" *Manang* Erleen asks excitedly as she sways her lithe supple body on the "catwalk" of my middle class condominium [beside Duncan Ramos's, my former Bedan student turned vocalist of the famous Southborder Band who just couldn't believe the new tenant picking her scattered eggs on the street was his odd college English professor, and now, they were to be neighbors!], along Matahimik Street, with the shanties of informal settlers nearby. My sister is wearing her old rose gown for my supposed December wedding.

*"Ang ganda ganda mo!* Stunning you!" I reply. My older sister is always a beauty to behold, magnificent, effervescent like no other. Her big eyes are ethereal, almost resembling the Blessed Virgin's loving eyes! Her natural bushy eyebrows are arched perfectly as those of the ancient Queen Cleopatra's in her small oval-shaped face. Her lips are lusciously pink that seem to pout and kiss at the same time while her cheeks are those of the enviable elegant aristocrat Hispanic. She has the nose, the neck, and shoulders of a well-poised fabulous modern queen or princess, a la Grace Kelly of Monaco. Her body is of a legendary nymph—virginal singing fresh, slender, graceful, with glowing skin, much fairer than any *porselanang kutis.* Her legs, oh, they are the fantastic long limbs of a Supermodel Of The World, not to mention her height of five eight. Her hair is silky smooth with the natural golden brown of our Spanish bloodline. My sister is a real *belladonna,* the uncontested runaway muse of the clan.

Today is the first week of December 2004. My church wedding with Enzo is scheduled on the 18th with elite Ateneo de Manila coming to Ilocandia!

*Manang* Erleen has always been my best friend, my confidant, my number one ally and moral booster, of course, my partner in crime. She eloped at seventeen with her smart *Atenista* boyfriend, the eldest son of an RTC Judge [belonging to the famous clan of Bello lawyers], who'd later become Justice of the Court of Appeals. I was their accomplice to the grand Romeo and Juliet forbidden plot, their elopement, and eventually, their civil wedding! I was fifteen years old, and came up with a nice little story [since my Religion teacher said everyone makes white lies especially when the situation calls for it! And this would torture my innocence then as to which white lies Popes say as they are human too! But I'd always console myself heaven is no lie!] to our very strict and unsuspecting father so he'd let me and my sister leave the house, with some *baon* of course. The rest is history. Her four bundles of joy came one after the other [three sons, one daughter]. I'd then live with them while I taught English, Journalism, and World Literature to high school girls, and ah, all those piles and piles of test papers to burn, oh to check!]. All those years were both fun Sister Acts and also tearful sister moments! She had her heartaches and woes, and I also had mine. We'd endlessly chat, first in good cheer, with both of us rolling on the floor in laughter, of course, with me farting endlessly [!], while her babes likewise tumbled on their baby mattresses in their ruffled manes and cute pyjamas with heavily sterilized bottles of milk stuck in their little mouths! Then much later, we'd both be blowing our noses and wiping our tears with the floral short sleeves of our *dusters* or of our old blouses in pastels or in the pleasant audacity of bright orange, yellow, and mint green, as we changed the babies' diapers! And all those sister bonding sessions were over good cups of hot coffee, cocoa, or tea, and or cold glasses of natural mango, pineapple, or *buko* juice, paired with either my sister's specialty pasta [spaghetti, lasagna, carbonara], or *Pinoy pancit bihon, canton, even pancit luglug* or *molo,* and on Sundays, cheese bacon omelettes and yummy pancakes, ending with her delectable mango crepes. Indeed, *Manang* Erleen was very much like our *Pinay* Castilian mother; they both looked angelic and even in their aprons! My sister can even make *katay* [butchering!] the unlucky goat by herself [!] in her so dainty kitchen that usually smelled of our *mestiza Mamang* Lourdes's kitchen while we were growing up in the heavenly bliss of Ilocos Sur! She also inherited our *Lilang's* signature recipes of *kilawin na ipon, kilawin na kambing, kilawin na pusit, kilawin na tirem* [oyster], *dinengdeng na saluyot at tinunong bangus, igado, adobo, dinuguan, paksiw na igat, lumpia, at bola-bola.* My sister was the perfect wife, mother, sister, and friend! Unfortunately, the hand of destiny had a mean plan for her that later on in her married life, she'd just cry her heart and soul silently, and at times, to me when I could snatch some time for my sister and my nephews and niece from the busyness of my life as an English and Applied Linguistics professor of both college and graduate students in the country's top Catholic university for the intellectual elite [Gosh, I had to flex my stubborn yet proudly Ilocano tongue every now and then for them so as not to be so marginalized [well, Howard Giles's Accommodation Theory of linguistic convergence!], you know that outcast feeling [!]and well, because most of that discourse community [not surprising!] would speak English in the Philippine acrolect [American twang or native-like variety!] of Dr. Lourdes Tayao, my UP professor, and I felt my mesolect seemed to be more of the basilectal in their midst, hence, my daily tongue exercises then before the mirror, causing most of my tardiness that I'd park my very dusty red Hyundai sedan right at the V.I.P.'s parking, before the Administration Building where the Mercedes, BMW's, and the rest of flashy cars were parked, and when I came back, there was already a free carwash promo offer on my windshield, including a free haircut! One time that I was running late to my class, the then varsity player, Fonacier, checked his watch as if to taunt me that I secretly wished he'd stumble on mud! The next time we met in the campus, oh, he was heavily bandaged, walking on leg-braces! Felt so guilty, naughty me!] aside of course from my roller coaster relationship with Enzo. I started to live on my own at the onset of my long joyful and stormy life with the man of my dreams but not without his baptism of fire from my older soulmate of a sister.

"Enzo, this is my *Manang* Erleen!" I nervously introduce my boyfriend of one week to my older sister while my little nephews and niece surround the now also nervous UP professor. It's almost lunch time. We are at IVS Marikina where I live with my sister and her family in their up and down decent apartment. My sister takes the extended hand of my boyfriend and smiles at him with a joke, "O, *ilang taon ka na?* Are you single? You seem to be double the age of Millie!" Enzo turns a little red, clears his throat, and gives her a straight answer, "*Manang*, I'm 45. I am marrying your sister!" Oh, the kids pull my boyfriend's sweaty hands, and ask for candies. I feel relieved! My sister goes back to the kitchen to prepare lunch while Enzo proceeds to the nearby *sari sari* store, with little chubby Diana Lyn, her small fat fingers in her mouth. The two come back with a gallon of rocky road ice cream. Sweet little incontrollable boys in colourful shorts and *sandos*, Earl and Caesar run towards them and grab the frozen delight while toddler Eloy Roman, with the thick curly lovable baby crop, coos in his playpen. Enzo laughs, with his wavy hair gently blown by the warm Marikina air, his signpen securely tucked in the pocket of his checkered polo, his signature artifacts! We then enjoy *sinigang na* Dagupan *bangus with fresh kangkong leaves, inihaw na baboy, kamatis at sibuyas* with Ilocos bagoong, and leche flan plus the rocky road; our first hearty lunch with an hors d'ouvre of jestful sarcasm together with soon, *Manang* Erleen's favorite *bayaw* [brother-in-law] in the making, for the next twelve years of her life.

"Mili, she has malignant tumor!" *Manong* Boy weeps on the phone, and my world is shattered. My brother-in-law, now a very successful litigation lawyer who'd later become Chairman and President of one of the country's most prestigious law firms, is crying incontrollably. My heartbeat races with time. My entire body is shaking, my vision blurred, I soon get my asthma, and I choke. Enzo is holding me tight, with tears in his eyes, and he's trembling too. He scampers for my inhaler. Today is February 2005. My beloved sister with whom much of my childhood dreams, secrets, and adventures had been spent and shared is dying with CANCER OF THE BRAIN! My wild rare blue orchid only has three more months to live. I get lost in the rage and shock of my soul. My heart is in pieces, smithereens of cruel, cruel pain! The family are all faces of that excruciatingly intense pain and woeful helplessness. *Papang* Eloy is silently crying as he gathers us outside the hospital room of *Manang* Erleen. Then he tells us in the voice of a grieving father, "We'll bury her in your *Mamang's* and *Lilang's* tombs." His tears fall one after the other, and takes out his blue-striped hanky to wipe them. *Manong* Elrey's eyes are sore red and he hugs our *Papang*. Our sisters, nephews, nieces, relatives, and the Bello family are all in tears. Eloy Earl, Diana Lyn, Eloy Caesar, and Eloy Roman are weeping silently beside their friends. I have become like a ticking timebomb. Enzo tries to make me drink the iced cold distilled water. My boyfriend is holding his rosary and Novena to Our Mother of Perpetual Help in one hand.

"*Gaga,* Mili, *ayanmon? Pardasam hahaha!*" *Manang* Erleen yells on me as we outrun each other in our stilettoes at the Sta. Lucia Carpark driveway. We just saw a late night movie, AMERICAN PIE 2 as the four Atenean brats have their own *gimiks* with their friends in different posh villages of the Metro. Enzo had late night class in UPD so he couldn't join us, though in most times that the family goes on malling, he's always carrying the large popcorn, coke, and my heavy big bag. "*Ala, adda ni Freddie ken Jason dita! hahaha!*" I yell back on my older pretty sister who's now obviously fagged out from the upward running. We found ourselves locked on the exit and entrance doors of a lower floor coming from the moviehouse so we had to take the almost perfectly circular driveway but upward!!! My sister's brand new CR-V, her husband's birthday gift, was parked at the rooftop! Oh, we both forgot for the movie just kept us laughing, breaking into shameless guffaws, and literally, pushing each other on our seats, with our cheese popcorn spilling all over, and hitting a couple of times the back of the seats of other moviegoers with our stomping crazy stilettoes!

*"Diak kayat, sikan ah ti gumatang! Mabainak!"* My beautiful sister pushes me hard towards the bargain seller's items displayed on a low table at the Quiapo overpass. She's in Fourth Year College, majoring in Industrial Psychology at Far Eastern University, our mother's Alma Mater. I am a college sophomore at the University of Santo Tomas. *"Pagbilhan nga po ng tawas*[local deodorizer] *para po sa ate ko!"* I whisper to the unmindful vendor as I point to my sister. *Manang* Erleen just couldn't stop pinching me with her long fingernails as I laugh and laugh at the middle of another busy day in the polluted but lively bursting city. This was in 1981.

*"O hala! Apay agan-anu ta* walking shoes mo? hahaha!" I tease my sister who's trying her best to hide the soap bubbles coming out of her brown footwear. We are on our way to the chapel for the Sunday afternoon mass in Guadalupe, Makati as her yet small family lives in Guadalupe BLISS housing project of the former Marcos government. My brother-in-law is still on his senior year at the Ateneo College of Law in Makati [serving as editor of their law journal and also as president of the student council], and my sister works as a medical representative at ELTA INDUSTRIES. But no matter how much my sister dives her shoes into big puddles of rain water, with her literally getting drenched in the now stronger rain, the soap bubbles just won't go away! Oh, how my lungs and my tummy got so painful from laughing so hard that my *Manang* Erleen swore she wasn't buying me any new panties and brassieres! But the next time I went to visit, riding that old red smelly bus from Forbes Street [now Lacson Street], she was excited to give me a new pair of metallic shoes!

*"Sige na,* read for me!" I'd plead and beg to my older sister to read to me the *BANNAWAG, LIWAYWAY, komiks,* WOMEN'S MAGAZINE, everything while I was around seven or eight years old. She'd give up saying no to me and soon reading out loud the printed words to her little sister

who's eagerly listening, her head with some fat lice on the lap of her ten year-old beautiful sister.

I slowly open the door. She looks at me, and asks if I have bought her a new lipstick, her favorite Belgian ice cream, and if I got her load for her celfone. I swallow my tears and proceed on the chair beside her hospital bed. I've got to do it no matter how I cursed fate for this unknown misery and woe. They said I had to do it. Nobody else would. No one else wanted. I look her in the eye. Her eyes are always beautiful. The Most Beautiful. But I've got to be one brave Indian war girl of my adventures in the sun. "You've got three months to live from today." I say the words like my little bows and arrows. My sister asks, "Why?" I answer, "*May bukol ka sa utak. Sa gitna.* It's malignant tumor." "*Diyos ko!* My God!" She says, and a single tear falls on her pretty face. I ran out of the room as fast as I could and buried my face on the chest of my crying Enzo. This episode in my life is one of the most painful that continues to haunt me up to this day!

My brother-in-law did everything he could to save and extend her life, his MOST BEAUTIFUL WIFE, ERLEEN BATIN-BELLO. Eight months were given from that harrowingly traumatic painful day I told my sister she had the worst type of malignant tumor right at the center of her brain, and it was too large, she'd die at an instant if they opened her head for surgery. But the other teams of doctors said she had a chance though a high risk. Her medical records were sent to top hospitals in the U.S. but they also had the same diagnoses and results. *Manong* Boy transferred my sister to a much more sophisticated local hospital in Quezon City. Days, weeks would pass with my dearest sister being taken in and out of the ICU. For a month or two, she'd seem much better, without any pains except that she'd crave for a lot of food, all her favorite meals and fine dinner[how she loved Peking duck and paella at Alba!]. Everyone did their best to give her everything she needed. We'd then have our last sister bonding moments of very painful conversations of whether she'd like to be cremated or just to be in her coffin 'til eternity, if the casket will be open to the family, friends, and relatives, as well as her greatest secrets, regrets, and biggest sins, making my heart palpitate and beat in the rhythm of a chopper's propeller! One afternoon, she asked me if I wanted her ghost to visit me every day and I didn't know how to answer her, so she said, she'd just be very discreet with her visits! She'd also describe to me what was going on in her pretty head, and how I'd bite my tongue and rush to the rest room to hide my tears when she'd gulp and swallow all those terrible capsules and meds though she was in great pain and difficulty, and when she'd tell me she wanted to squeeze her brain in the television! Then the four kids started to stay away for some days, weeks; not wanting to go home early. I was feeling that way too but I had to battle it out. My beautiful sister's silky hair started to disappear, then her face started to look a little different, her long perfect legs were turning into a stranger's, her fabulous body getting bigger by the day, with her stomach becoming like an unwanted mass of ball, her regal shoulders, neck, and flawless milky skin getting and bearing those ugly violets, spreading like ghastly maps of horrible places, then she'd squeal little and big secrets of visiting friends and their spouses with them fighting on the spot in my sister's bedroom[!], and worst, she began to talk and babble like a toddler for she was at this time losing all control of her brain since the malignant tumor was way too monstrous in the last months! She'd then claim to be seeing our dead loved ones [our *Lilang*, our *Mamang*, our sister-in-law, *Ate* Grace fetching her, including crying angels, and the horrifying devil himself who carried a huge sickle with his big horns, long tail, and ugly guffaws !]! I cried and cried and cried out loud to the heavens, to all the angels and saints, to Mama Mary, to Jesus! I wept no end each day I saw what was happening to my *Manang* Erleen! Then he came. THE GOOD JESUIT.

"Ma'am, this is Fr. Manny Flores, SJ." My very kind Jesuit seminarian student in my English 12 class, Stephen from Myanmar, introduces me to the good-looking fair-complexioned tall and muscular smiling priest. "Hello po Fr. Manny. I'm Millie." I take the warm handshake of the good-natured Director of the International Jesuit Formation in the Philippines, and uncle of two famous former child actors at the time [Antonette Taus and her brother, more popularly remembered as *Cedie*. It was odd that much much early on, I'd feel very strangely one day I met Antonette at the Ateneo campus!]. From that day on, the Jesuit priest and the Ateneo de Manila English professor would drive almost everyday after class and even on weekends from Loyola Heights to Village East, Cainta, Rizal, braving the daily rush hour traffic, with light to serious and out of this world conversations as the good Jesuit would then discover of my special gift of clairvoyance and that third eye! He'd recommend for me to see the famous Fr. Bulataw, S.J. so he could help me develop more "the gift!" Of course, I thought otherwise as I've always been very secretive and private with my other worlds! Fr. Manny would then hear my very sick and dying sister's venial and mortal sins, celebrate the Holy Mass right there in the *sala*, in *Manang* Erleen's bedroom, even in her hospital rooms whenever she had to be confined, give her the anointing of the sick, all the sacraments. The good Jesuit priest would also carry my sister to the second floor of my new MADASALIN STREET apartment where I started to live in with my now husband, Enzo or Enzo. At the time, my husband was in school, and I requested my brother-in-law to allow me to take care of my sister for three days right there in our apartment. She seemed to be very fine, and I wanted to just be with her. Fr. Manny, being a karate blackbelt, managed to bring my very heavy sister up to our bedroom which was the only airconditioned room. He also went out in the neighbourhood asking for ice as *Manang* Erleen needed a lot of the ice cubes to ease the pains of her thighs, legs, and feet; she'd request and beg to be rolled over and over on the floor! People would then recognize the Jesuit priest and he'd come back with a lot of stuff. I'd cook our simple meals with Fr. Manny always cheerful, helpful, and patient. He'd also teach me a very special prayer! The entire family loved him. We always do. I always will.

The combined chemotheraphy and radiation given to *Manang* Erleen helped her to last eight months. Enzo and I had to get married ASAP! We were supposed to be wed by our town mayor December 18, 2004 but the papers did not prosper yet so the farm civil wedding had to be cancelled, with me sending so many text messages to my colleagues in Ateneo [Josie Lacson, and Rachel, thank you for all the assistance and love!], informing them of the sad development. Several had made their transportation and hotel reservations early, aside from all those we reserved so Enzo and I felt so bad, ashamed, and dismayed. At the time, December 2004, *Manang* Erleen was still very much in the pink of health except for her allergies on her legs and arms which would come and go with her medication and ointments. She'd drive here and there, from Manila to Ilocos and back together with her family. One dusk of that December, she came walking, alone, from our other family house at the foot of Sleeping Beauty to our house [Enzo's and mine]. The moon was so large, so low, and it looked like a huge fireball! I will never forget how I felt that moment I saw my beloved sister walking so prettily under that ugly ball of blood! When Enzo and I were married by Judge Yadao in Quezon City Hall, April 19, 2005, my dearest sibling was just taken back home to Village East, Cainta from the hospital where she had her daily radiation and chemotherapy. That was why Enzo and I just wore our old clothes except for my fuchsia shawl that I would later spread on the chest and shoulders of my beautiful dead sister whom I've loved so much and will forever love! *Manang* Erleen was still able to attend my church wedding with her on the wheelchair, not wearing her old rose gown as she was quite big at this time. When she died on 5 October 2005, in her hospital room [where I almost hurled Edgar Allan Poe's cursed fate upon that lady neurologist who recommended to my brother-in-law, euthanasia for my dying sister [!], with the good Jesuit and my well-mannered Uncle Roland stopping me from my berserk of *mano-a-mano* with that unbelievable brain specialist!], I had her wear in her coffin her old rose gown that she happily promenaded in my condominium, December 2004. I then resigned from the prestigious Ateneo de Manila University despite the fact that my security of tenure was already to be given me in two weeks' time from my sister's death. My pain was too deep, and my world was shattered. A year after, in 2006, I applied and competed for a Fulbright Scholarship Grant to Harvard University to do research on academic and creative writing as I remembered in one of my afternoons of reflection, how Fr. Bien Nebres, SJ, the sitting President of Ateneo de Manila in the five years I was with the university, would encourage me one lucky morning, to pursue higher grounds for my writing, publication and research, saying he believed in me, with both of us graduating from public schools for our elementary education, and hailed from Ilocandia. I made it to the Short List, but ultimately lost the opportunity as the panel said, I've not taught creative writing yet. A month later, Frank T. Villa together with his family was then sent to me by Fr. Manny Flores, SJ in our MADASALIN STREET apartment for me to help write his biography. Hence, I wrote the biographical book, 75 YEARS OF JOURNEYING IN GOD'S GRACE while still mourning the death of my wild rare blue orchid, my loving, my eternally beautiful sister, *Manang* Erleen.

*Chapter Four*

---

# The Cage Cleaners of Jerusalem: Phantom of Eternity

"…SO THE CHILDREN OF ISRAEL made all the work…and, behold, they had done it as the Lord had commanded, even so had they done it…"[Exodus 39:42-43]. "Mama, it's 5:30. *Gising ka na.* You've got class in UST." I open my eyes and see the gentle, handsome face and loving eyes of my husband. "Papa, ten minutes more." My eyes close again. "This is usually what happens every morning in our home; the dramatics of my poor sleeping habits. Mama, it's six a.m. *Ma-traffic na naman tayo.* Your hot bath is ready." Enzo gently caresses and strokes my back and shoulders. "Papa, I'm not feeling well!" I turn my back once more on my husband and continue sleeping. Since I was a kid, getting up early has always been tough as my chronic insomnia began that early in my life that our granny, *Lilang* Andang would announce both the river and the mountains were on big fire, burning wild all the trees and the fish, to get me up on my feet! Back in high school, I'd then be joyfully picking the candy wrappers in the campus quadrangle for being tardy while my classmates were already taking the quizzes. This school tardiness episode would get my exhausted government executive father bringing me to Vigan unscheduled, scolding me all the way as all my siblings would have gone early to school with me still dreaming on my doubledeck! By the time I reach school, the very strict St. Paul nun would then be on the look out for the latecomers with her little stick, hence, finding myself hiding behind the big wooden doors, with my black shoes exposed! Alas, the little whipping [Sr. must be thinking then of God's caveat to use the rod so as not to spoil the late comer, oh, the child!] of my trembling legs before the joy of picking the litter of angels! Enzo has gotten used through the years to the terrible sleeping habit of his much younger wife. I later wake up to see my husband and our little son, JP feeding our pets, with Linda wagging her tail in glee as she eats her fish and newly cooked white rice while our cats purr endlessly as they eagerly wait for the generous ration of their breakfast. Kitty is as quiet and patient as always. An exception to the entire feline kingdom. She is her Royal Highness. I proceed to the *sala* of our housing unit and watch the morning program. My chest is heavy. I still have that bad asthma which got my *mag-ama* again brushing my feet the night before, each foot with their own strokes to get that blood circulating, helping me to breathe much better. My husband knows too well how to operate the nebulizer, and the dose of medicine to give me with three year-old JP assisting him. Almost every night, my nocturnal asthma sends my husband and son scampering for the brush, the nebulizer, and the meds. I acquired my bronchial asthma from my very taxing teaching loads, moonlighting in two to three colleges or universities aside from my full-time teaching job while I was still single. Cosmopolitan existence and lifestyle plus the M.A. and Ph.D. studies were really costly [a decent apartment would cost ten thousand pesos!], so I had to work like the Philippines' beast of burden, the carabao! Well, even now as the bills just keep coming plus the precious toys [mostly from Shoppersville, long before it got burned!] of the little angel that should keep him happy and safe while playing! Thank God, he loves little books too, much of my husband's influence for he keeps so many of these tiny print wonders in his old knapsack! With the fine warm ray of morning sunlight coming in through the old big windows of Dutch architecture, JP runs to me in his printed pyjamas and plants on my face his little angelic kisses. He proudly tells me he's got new twin kittens from Sheila, our very meek white cat but with also the bad cat asthma as she often vomits especially when the rice is too soft or *mabato*. My husband then brings me a hot cup of ginseng tea, courtesy of his kind Korean student [my thoughtful and sweet Chinese and Korean students too would bring me all those heavenly ginseng, special teas!], and my breakfast of fried eggs, corned beef, and *sinangag*. Enzo never fails to wake up early to cook our breakfasts, prepare our hot baths, feed the pets, and clean our vehicles [his Sylvester Stallone and my Red Bull, both old by this time!]. Our home in the metropolis is very simple yet we are more than content and happy even when we'd clean our cats'cages every day of our lives, whether it's a sunny day or a rainy day, a busy day or a lazy weekend, even on Christmas eve and new year! Enzo just got used into waking up each morning with a lot of the "diamonds "of our now thirty feline [each in their colourful cages lined up in our hallway to the kitchen and our living room], and of our Labrador for him to clean with his big diligent hands, his agile body, and kind good heart. My cleaning schedule is mostly at night or on weekends. Enzo also becomes such an effective veterinarian, giving our sick feline biogesic, paracetamol, diatabs, hydrite, vitamins, etc., and Good Lord [!], they'd be up again on all fours! JP would help his Papa every now and then by carrying his own dipper of water to clean the kittens' little cage. The father and son team is a joy to behold especially when they are not fighting over some spilled cat ration, and hilarious sight indeed when the little monster runs around the house in his small pyjamas being chased by his peeved 62-year old father as the mischievous cherub has just made *sundot* [poke!] of his father's behind! The little one might have gotten his mother's naughtiness who'd *siko* or elbow her snoring husband or cover his mouth with her laughing hands at night. Yes, there's so much fun, there's so much joy, and there are also plenty of trials, hardships, and responsibilities, including oddities in our family life.

"Oh my God!" I make the sign of the cross as I see a headless man seated at the porch of our neighbour by past six in the evening. I'm reminded of the headless figurine of the groom on the cake of my church wedding with my husband, Enzo! I've wrapped and hidden the figurine from him since our wedding night upon my discovery of its frightful omen! St. Joseph's head too unfortunately broke when the wind cast its fury one night and the dining room's windows in Ilocos were still open. We have just moved today to our new place. This is 2010. Enzo is 62 years old, his hair still thick and wavy though there's more of the grizzled. But he's as strong, as alert, as energetic and *maliksi* as ever. He's quite fit, the strength of a man in his forties. The years have not taken away the luster and enigma in his eyes, the charm in his smile, the oozing sex appeal, the oomph in his ways, gait, and persona. I am as madly in love with my husband as the first time he smiled at me! And he is more than caring and loving, in fact, he has totally spoiled me, thus, I've become a real spoiled wife, a brat of a wife! And he has done so with our three year old child, Joseph Mary Peter Paul Lamb [Enzo Anselmo Mary the Blessed], that he's now a little brat! However, we three human members of our extended household, with our feline and canine would just spend the rest of our complete family life in the perfect bliss and also, the inevitable blisters of destiny.

"Sheila, oh my God, Sheila! Stop! Stop running! Papa, Papa! Where are you? Sheila is getting away! Hurry!" I scream at the top of my lungs while I try to chase Sheila as she struts so fast from our living room to the street. Enzo runs ahead of me and calls out on Sheila, the fugitive cat of the day! Yes, every day, some feline would get so playful as they'd attempt to tour the campus! Oh, Sheila stops running right at the gate of our nice neighbors' home, with the matriarch, a very religious woman, her tall, friendly, *mestizo* husband a former military who's turned excellent English editor. They have a very kind English speaking handsome Muslim son-in-law, whose two younger sons would sometimes come to our house and play with JP while I'd cook for them some *merienda*. One time, I served them Purefoods hotdogs. The two cute little Muslim boys said, "Oh sorry *po*, but we don't eat pork. Our religion does not allow it. Do you have beef instead?" I was delightfully amused and amazed for the impressive eloquence and candidness of the little Allahs and searched my refrigerator for the precious beef. Unfortunately, Enzo could not eat *baka* because of his high blood pressure and heart ailment, and his cardiologist has put him on lifetime medication, so no beef, not even a piece of *charqui* or a slice of *charolais* in our usual menu, and oh, no *tapa* or beef steak for our polite English speaking little Muslim neighbors, both with long silky hair and handsome *mestizo* faces but whose first names are very *Pinoy*. Hence, I just gave them candies as they ran around with my little JP, struggling with a few English words to hold cute conversations with his older *Englisero* playmates while he likewise teaches them his growing exuberant *matalinghagang* [meaningful] Filipino idioms, with no less than Professor Enzo Q. Quiambao [one of the staunch champions for the intellectualization and propagation of the national language, and wrote the college hymn of the UP College of Education] for his father and mentor, teaching him all the *bugtong* [riddles], and *maikling kwentos* [short stories]every day, especially at bedtime. At times, I'd feel an outcast when my two boys would be bantering in those exquisite nuances and truly proudly *Pinoy* tongue, the *Pambansang Dila!* I'd then bring out my own esoteric and quintessential mother tongue of the brave hardworking and thrifty [*kuripot!*] Ilocanos! Whoa! Every feline and our canine, Mary Nazarene Paula Erlinda Cassiopeia would purr and bark in the multilingual multi-cultural home, and Beauty, the largest of the feline kingdom starts to explore more diverse homes in the wonderful chartreuse of the neighborhood one time that we were gladly haggling with the *tinderas* and *tinderos* in the *tiangges*. Until much later on, Beauty turns nidifugous, prefers to be transient in our home by wringing out her humongous body out of her pretty brand new pink cage, as perhaps, she gets to be more versatile and becomes real polyglot as she goes around and mingle with the pets of every neighbour. Unfortunately, extroverted Beauty gets to walk into "landmines," or enemy lines on several occasions.

The din of some unruly kingdom flies high and sharp in the air. It's around six p.m., December 2010. I'm busy decorating the kitchen. I've just finished, some three weeks ago, putting up our trees [one old but too special as it was Enzo's gift to me in the late 90's with the singing Christmas lights and a fat dancing singing Santa but which later on sulked and corroded!], and the other, very new from the *tiangge*. My two boys of course were very helpful, with JP handing me the big and small glittering and shiny balls, and my husband putting the Christmas star on top of our trees, the Filipino tradition and custom. All three of us basked [as usual!] in the joys of the coming yuletide, hanging the cute smaller red, green, yellow, and white *parol* by the windows even in our toilet [!], the dancing Christmas lights at the facade of our old light green three-bedroom house, leaving the arrangement and easthetics to my quite eccentric and funny husband with the three year-old angel helping him come up with an abstract painting [!] of Christmas lights, Jesus Christ! The community would then pass by our house with obvious amused smiles, the younger ones would giggle, whisper to one another, and break into careless guffaws, pissing me off to eternity, chasing them with my broom especially when my back, my waist, or my entire human anatomy was but too exhausted from clearing and cleaning the whole of some 800 square meters of dried *santol*, bamboo, and mango leaves, including overriped fruits! Tonight, two weeks before Christmas Eve, I'm giving my kitchen the colors and the feel! While the cool green Christmas curtains are up and hanging festive on those huge Dutch windows, there are walls and corners that remain bare of the season's spirit, trappings, and trimmings. My obsession for fine arts and interior design makes me too excited for the night! I must hurry with the supper of *tinola*, thankful indeed that Enzo and JP were able to buy fresh *malunggay* [horse tree] at the Cooperative or Coop beside the Shopping Center [In Ilocos, we just go to our backyard to get *marunggay* fresh and right from their trees! Enzo planted two of the tallest in the entire compound as we live close to the four other houses of my siblings; it was only *Manang* Erleen who had their house built in the city.]. Both boys are now busy bantering in the bedroom by the tall and pliant Bamboo trees and a huge Carabao Mango tree, turning the room, the bed, and the linens into a total chaos of tickles, wrestling tournament, big and little laughs! But, I just let them be [as that is their usual evening ritual!] while the chicken broth fills the evening air, the cages beginning to shake with the wide awake and waiting lovely and gentle four legs of purring golden browns, blacks, and whites. Linda Cassiopeia likewise starts to fill the night with her pleasant and patient barking. We've always found our Labrador exceptionally kind and gentle like Her Royal Highness, our oldest cat, Kitty. Both are the very special legendary heads of our menagerie! Once the entire household is full and content with the good chicken and the fresh greens, and our hands have dutifully cleaned the colourful cages with the green serpent-like long hose of generous water, and our dog has been given her nightly tour and walk, my husband and little child prepare to sleep while I stay behind in the kitchen to prim her up. Whoossshhh, ahhhhh! The war goddess, *Enyo* suddenly whishes, groans, and grunts by our roof, door, and windows, and the rather peaceful and delightful evening turns into a night of unprecedented agony! A casbah establishes itself so haughtily and condescendingly in the geographical verdure of our paradise, and Lord Milton writes of his "Paradise Lost..." None of the heavenly bodies forewarned me or did they? But Hesperus persisted to console our home, our *charpoys* of fun and contentment though our golden apples seemingly have lost the watch of the lovely Hesperides from hereon!

The nasal baritone voice stops my scissors from merriment. My pre- Christmas excitement fades unceremoniously. I hear my husband's voice thundering in anger for the very first time as he has always been soft spoken, well-mannered decent man, with that distinct chariness so admirable among the descendants of Adan! I've not noticed he has taken his noble sword of battle to deal with the overbearing mythical *Bellona or Discordia*. Oh, hereupon this night, our family would then be put to the test, to the terrible raging fire, as we trek unfamiliar grounds, foreboding tracks, the frightening wilderness...

THE BAPTISM OF THE FAVORED LITTLE CHILD OF MISCHIEF! The following Sunday of December 2011 is the delayed christening of our only child. Our dearest friends, including several of my UST graduate students are with us to grace and celebrate the occasion. Our big family in Ilocos would then have a separate celebration with our small family of three, plus some 29 feline, and Linda Cassiopeia. Oh, Fr. Ubaldus Djonda, SVD officiates the event and Holy Mass. He's my M.A. student in English Language Studies, a very smart, good-natured, and kind-hearted Indonesian priest, who speaks Filipino like a local, having finished his scholastic priestly studies in Tagaytay. Fr. Uz has become a family to us, even travelling from the city to Ilocandia to welcome with us the coming of a new year, and with him saying beautiful Holy Mass at the old rose terrace of our dreams, and oh, giving as well the final blessing to our dead cat, naughty playful Golgol which suffocated, with the good priest controlling so hard and tactfully his amusement! My dear old friend, Charlie Veric, poet and now, successful author, has just returned from his Ph.D. studies in Yale, while fabulous chanteuse *Manang* Cori Quitoriano-Perez, *Manang* Erleen's high school classmate in St. Paul Vigan, has come in her flowing green slacks, with her sweet charms and elegant wit, a Fulbright scholar who studied the Ilocano variety of the Hawaii-based *Iloko*. Both were my colleagues, my closest and walking comrades in Loyola, with whom I've shared much of my joys, my tears, and my dreams. Retired UP Professor and former PALT President, Ma'am Teresita Ignacio, former UPD Guidance Counselor, Dr. Benilda Lascano, and UP COE Professor Elenita Que [whispering to my husband why he is now offering in the mass the bottle of wine given to him as Christmas gift!] are also around to serve as godparents of our very playful cherub who's wearing a long-sleeved little *Barong Tagalog*. My good old friends during my San Beda days are in full force as well as my sweet old colleagues in SMC, QC. Of course, our dearest *Ninang* Nonette Corpuz is giving the eloquent and inspiring speech and blessing for the three year old little cherub who just won't sit in one place, with *Manang* Cori helping me and Enzo to keep still inside the *Simbahan Ng Tuklong* of Christ The King, Quezon City. My very special friend, Victoria "Vicky" Carbonnel [the smart, charming, and bubbly emcee during our church wedding] who's with her handsome boyfriend, and later, her loving husband, is joyfully reprimanding the little boy to stop running here and there and in the entire compound of the chapel as Jesus, she tells my child, is more than dizzy with his endless running [Rest in peace my dear friend!]. Sweet Sr. Henrietta Gomez, a UST Ph.D. Psychology and Guidance and Counseling student from Bangladesh just cannot control her giggles as little JP keeps annoying his guests especially his now tired but excited parents; likewise, a dozen young seminarian SVD's smiling and laughing like the most good-looking of happy saints! The beautiful soprano, Irene Quiso-Ednave of the internationally acclaimed UST Singers, and her Guitar Major husband, Ryan of the UST Conservatory of Music [who'd later teach guitar lessons to the wealthy and royal Brunei kids] render the event most lovely singing and music, wonderful, wonderful memories my heart will always keep and reminisce with that incomparable sweet smile on my lips! The good cheerful company of mostly, if not all educators proceeds then to a cozy Chinese restaurant along Timog Avenue, and continues the festive, jubilant rejoicing and celebration of the Holy Baptism of the incontrollable but much-loved three year-old only child of Enzo and Millie. "Welcome Joseph Mary Peter Paul Lamb "JP" Batin Quiambao to the Christian world," says the all too glad aspergillum while it generously sprinkles the holy water on the angel of mischief!

THE WILDERNESS OF TEMPTATION AFTER THE SACRAMENT OF BAPTISM Our overflowing joy from the baptismal rite and luncheon party for our little one turns sour the following day for the biggest and strongest blows in our family life would then come to test our patience, humility, and faith. These painful trials and ordeals would shake the foundations of our home, the marriage that binds me and my husband, including our sense of, faith and devotion. We really never expected anything like it, the persecution that would come like a destructive gust of heat, the beginning of my years of intense personal struggle, of our family's pains and agony, of our unspeakable burden and misery, as well as our endless battles with sin for about seven years! It's like going up with the newly baptized JESUS to that dreadful hill in the Judean Desert, with intense bullying, hauling mercilessly all of its might to pound me and my family into dust and to nothingness! Almost every day of my life, of our family life is now attacked, vexed, and inveighed with the harsh CULTURE OF BULLYING! I would then seek that little Indian war girl of my childhood to help me and my home! But human nature as it is, finds its fallen side more than tempting, overpowering the good in men. Anger indeed dehumanizes, and makes the ugliest beasts in each one; nobody wants to lose in the senseless war game! Soon, the Acacia trees would witness how the once tree climbing little Indian war girl would battle nasty *Enyon, Discordia, and Bellona,* unyielding to their on-rush and cunning foray of despiteous langue, shielding her home from the slew of vexatious, calumnious tongue! But, spite, at its worst, just won't stop to cleave, dig, and ruin the joy of the Cage Cleaners' home. The oral defamation would then become like sheafs of the cursed plant, yet clandestinely spatters to scourge, agonize, persecute, sentence, and nail on the cross a human being or fellow human beings. All because of hurt ego, wrong presumption, rash judgment, and more so, because of the culture of persecution, the culture of abuse, the culture of bullying, that has sadly infested, plagued, and besieged what is supposedly an inherently good, exuberantly jovial, loving, and rich native culture!

Since time immemorial, sin and mores have always gripped humanity in such conflict and paranoia, in such intensity and scorn, in great tension and attention, as well as enormous interest for the Holy Bible itself takes off its invaluable lessons and parables right from the story of Adan and Eve, and their commission of man's original sin. Yes, men and their sins! The parable of the first stone for anyone without sin is the greatest reminder of how one human being should deal with the sin of another human being. Through the ages, societies would create their laws and codes to regulate human conduct, attempting to define what is morally good and morally acceptable. However in so doing, there are lives that get destroyed or ruined especially when processes and procedures lack discernment, enlightened judgment, true religion, and genuine faith in God. How human nature would castigate its own shadow, glare, and snare as it struggles with its too many offenses, crimes, and burdens. The overly self-righteous overlooks the Commandments and the Beatitudes, becomes too stingy, punitive, hostile, and indifferent to the misery of the already miserable; as if human suffering didn't scourge the soul, and didn't render the spirit restless! As generally observed in the Philippine islands, the tendency to inflict undue pain or misery to others has evolved into an alarming culture of bullying, growing fast and widely pervasive, seeping into any discipline, cutting through the social classes, afflicting all age brackets [that's why the recent laws against it in schools and in the workplace but none yet at the *Barangay* or neighbourhood and community life that even in the far-flung *barrios*, rural bullies are now on board the gruesome or repulsive status quo!]. As viewed by social and political scientists, this sad development runs contrary to the nation's attempts to bring itself to a global or world class sophistication and civilization. Very ironic indeed that instead of using vision, good education, powerful voice, great talent, and superb abilities and skills to buoy up, nurture, and harness progressive individual and collective energy towards pro-active inclusive embracing transformative change, these are but wasted, and distorted to literally truncate, obfuscate, and cut the lines, in favor for the hate culture, the despotic culture leading to absolutism, which in world history, for so many many years and hitherto, has borne legions of darkness, the anti-Christ, tyrants, oppressive dictators, and now, international terrorists instead of good prophets, empowered laity and societies, visionaries, and dynamic prime movers! But then again, wasn't Jesus Christ the greatest victim of persecution, today's bullying, thousands of years ago? Indeed, the social evil has long been around! At present, bullying has evolved and morphed considerably largely threatening and too massively dangerous, assuming the form of terrorism [the generic!], and its clones of political, economic, cultural, social, and moral! Truly terrifying and largely threatening to global or world peace, to national security, to family life and personal bliss. Adopting a more radical look into the new face of present day war, terrorism seems to sprout and thrive faster on soil that is trampled upon thus, positivism, respect for human and sovereign rights, empowerment, social equity, philanthropy, and compassion should take the upperhand as early and as quickly to quash a brewing seething anger, wrath, and fury! For instance, farmers and fishermen should be adequately guided, supported, and empowered to till the land for the good abundant harvests as well as fish safely, peacefully, and confidently for the *sinigang na bangus, inihaw na panga ng tuna, kilawin na ipon, binatukang kuhol, pinadapang alimango, at kinamatisang pla pla!* Violence, in all its forms, like bullying, undoubtedly begets violence as human nature is inclined to the law of reciprocity or even mutuality in all of its principle! That's why CRITICAL ENLIGTHENED DISCOURSES should be allowed to take root and prefonderate in no time! Moral compass can never lead to sainthood unless it purges itself from too much fear, enmity or ill-will! What unforgivable failure then of the "groves of academe," of good quality education to miss or eschew to address and apprehend the asperity of the new face of *Discordia* or anarchy [bullying!], and its unbridled, unchecked, or tolerated arrogance for such behaviour, and mindset or mental state escalates into the worst type of modern day sophisticated violence---TERRORISM! The modern conundrum should be dealt with the timeless wisdom of Confucius [DO NOT DO UNTO OTHERS WHAT YOU DO NOT WANT OTHERS DO UNTO YOU], and of course, overarchingly, the teaching of Jesus, LOVE THY NEIGHBOR! Sadly, few seem to care or bother with the real deep wounds of humanity! Like the cries of families of victims of medical malpractice that fall on deaf ears or indifferent societies, and henceforth, the medical malpractitioners continue committing more crimes, with them turning into the most dangerous of homo sapiens for they do not get punished nor held accountable for their terrible offense. Apparently, the medical code of ethics is used to cover their tracks and crimes, declaring them innocent despite the glaring offense or malpractice. Such case appears to be the most sophisticated of today's forms of bullying [of the trusted specialist to the all-trusting lay man!], of today's faces of violence, of today's variants of sophisticated terrorism [for how can the lay man argue with the doctor of medicine, backed up by the formidable medical code of ethics which not a single other doctor of medicine would dare touch and question?]. How social ills depict human wretchedness, the glaring institutional faux pas, and the angst in souls! That's why it's best to read memoirs ["75 Years of Journeying in God's Grace," "BLAZING LIGHT...In The Grace Of One Journey," "THE CAGE CLEANERS OF JERUSALEM," and not to forget my prayer book and likewise poetry, LOST IN EREBUS...THE LONGEST PRAYER] to get the chance to stop one's nonchalant personal clock and nourish the needy human heart, mind, and soul. Sin, at this time and age, is apparently a diminishing return of too much sophistication in lifestyle, alienation from one's roots, identity crisis [not knowing the real self, failure to understand or respect uniqueness or the otherness from the other], and confusion as to life's purpose, most importantly, one's true essence, one's humanity. So, it's good to sit by the porch, in the garden under a nice tree or even on its boughs with the little memoirs, and allow oneself to journey with fellow human beings on the roads to joy, peace, and salvation, of course, with some shedding of tears in between guilt and delight, anguish and bliss, wretchedness and glory. I honestly believe a company or congregation of remorseful sinners and penitent pilgrims gets the bonus of sure sainthood likewise for more, not just limited to a chosen few! It's more like, birds of the same feather pray and become saints among eagles, barbets, fulmars or among ravens together!

THE TRAIL OF PURIFICATION, THE JOURNEY TO BETHLEHEM. Our "Scourging At The Pillar" was not however without its purifying saving grace no matter how close to desperadoes or yobboes we have been [especially in my case] in those years of tears and seasons of woe; it came gradually together with the weight of the Cross in the highs and lows of our family life, of married life, of being a husband, a wife, and as parents to our child. While almost every day would see me aim my slingshot to the shebang and frivolous couture of sinful tongues, deep within me something unusual was taking place. It was like my own sins were being washed by my own routine, my chores, my duties, my responsibilities. I was able to do a lot, so much that in spite of my miseries, I was able to overcome myself, survive the great burden with all those blisters and wounds, and focus on my home though the ordeal was truly devastatingly onerous, scarring my innermost being! OUR AGONY IN THE GARDEN as a persecuted family likewise tested the courage and faith of my husband, bestowing upon him the Grace of Stewardship as he learned how to be the Good Shepherd and Servant of God in the harrowing and tormenting times of living, both in the Light and in Darkness. I've always felt my husband had this purifying grace coming to him in almost the same way as it did to me, except of course, that he was to be both the firm yet loving husband and "father" to me for my then ethical vagary, my vagrant soul, and ill roguish volatile temperament, not to mention his trying and difficult role to be both doting yet disciplinarian father to our mischievous *unico hijo*. The Blessing Grace for our little son came in a much lighter cross as he was just but a child though he learned early the meaning of the words, bullying, bullies, and HOW IT FEELS TO BE BULLIED. Yes, some unexplainable thing was happening and we were not fully aware, neither did we really understand, as if we climbed Mt. Arbel with its numerous dangerous high cliffs then trekked to Mt. Precipice to share or endure in the rejection of THE SON, and to Mt. Tabor to witness a miraculous glorious event! But the TRAIL was there...

KITTY. She led us and her loyal court, with our Mary Nazarene Paula Erlinda Cassiopeia, to a Purifying Burning Saving Grace. She brought us to a "manger." She took us on that TRAIL that came close to THE HOLY MANGER. She gave us JERUSALEM while we lived in joy and in tears. For seven years of our lives...

From that stormy night that she walked like a most regal queen into our *sala,* in our simple home, on the eve of my husband's 62nd birthday, our lives were never the same again. She brought with her a most extraordinary royal court, the rest of our feline that came like a throng of nobility with the purest of hearts as well as with their great mission. Our one and only canine that came from the holy women of St. Paul Of Chartres gladly welcomed each one with her gentle barking, unthreatening, and protectively affectionate. Our Labrador made them feel so at home and joined their noble cause. Each day and night that followed had our hands full of real burden and kept them dirty with all the waste, the "diamonds, the gems" of our pets though of overwhelming, inexplicable joy! But while our hands were dirty and smelly, the house with the zoo feel and air, our hearts and souls were being purged from our own sinfulness, our faults, our shortcomings. As we'd wash our pets' cages, our offenses seemed likewise to be taken away, with our hearts and souls unburdened, cleansed by the purifying "WATER" of Divine Mercy and love! While we were bullied and persecuted day and night, in weeks, months, and years, our home never succumbed, never gave up to the billowing waves and the rough waters; its core, its pith remained strong, brave, and steadfast, as if the Holy Blood of Jesus poured out upon the three of us, draped and covered us with Overflowing and Burning Love! The joy was unceasing, the faith immense, the love genuine! As if there was a constant fireplace that exuded immeasurable warmth to our agitated hearts, a great bonfire that perked our spirits in the coldest emptiest nights, candles that never ran out of glow, a perfect sheen no darkness could ever enshroud with fear, encouraging us to keep holding on, believing, and waiting on God's promises. Our home refused to be beaten by the odds, our spirits unyielding, were never crushed nor broken even when the tempests seemed to be more and endless, even when our roof literally leaked a lot and threatened to fall! Husband, wife, and child just wouldn't stop living in the Grace of Joy, in the Grace of Hope, in the Grace of Simple Life. We'd just be laughing like little kids while we'd get soaked in the rain as we'd carry big and small basins, old and new pails, running here and there, shouting cheerfully to remind each other to be careful while getting rid of the rain water! My husband became even more responsible, hardworking, and humble. He'd wash morning and evening each bowl, each drinking cup with his patience and meek heart, though these were filled with pet's waste, from time to time. Of course, he had his gloves and his boots, including his mask but the grub, brunt, and burden were never for the lazy man nor for the arrogant intellectual neither for the uncaring indifferent husband and father nor for the unfeeling cruel human. But he was ENZO, the faith, the face, and courage like of JOSEPH, the hands and work similar to JOB, the obedience and all-trusting submission to God's word of Abraham! While he'd fret and frown on certain days, he'd still go about his DUTY as a CAGE CLEANER. Oh, how I loved him more whenever I'd see his tall frame and back bent low, feeding lovingly and patiently each of our feline, and while cleaning each cage, holding the long green hose that he'd carefully keep on the left side of our house, drenched in both perspiration and cleaning water, as well as whenever he was squatting or sitting on a stool, washing and wiping with a soft dry cloth each of our cats' eating and drinking bowls and cups. Those moments painted a perfect picture of an accomplished man yet had no qualms of the ordinary man's grubby, menial, dirty work! Such days and nights reflected the kindness, the genuine goodness of his heart, and how roses would be strewn in the pathways of greatness, shining not in the palaces of the mighty and boastful but in a little corner where the most beautiful, diligent, dutiful hands work in all humility and devotion! Such a lowly, humble corner glittered with the opal in my eyes, the Goodness of a True Servant of Christ, and how that LIGHT diffused to soften, melt, and pacify the angry troubled heart when days were but tales of disillusion, agitation, and disenchantment! My husband would selflessly, lovingly, patiently do these hard LABOR, routine, and chores most of the time while I and our little son were watching t.v. or while we were still fast asleep! Enzo had his sins just like each and everyone. But what made him more special were his immense HUMILITY, impeccable DISCIPLINE, and valiant ZEAL to do what was needed to be done even if this was menial or burdensome task, even if he wanted to just lie down and sleep, even if taunting mocking eyes were on him! Even when the bullying was at its worst! He had a strong sense of DUTY, and the admirable readiness to SACRIFICE, obedient to the dictates and rules of hard labor, submitting himself to the Grace of Silent Suffering! And he truly loved our pets as if they were all his children! His soft spoken, kind, congenial, and gentlemanly but resilient ways would help him unfailingly to surmount the incessant and harsh blows of life. I knew I was a very difficult woman, a notoriously spoiled wife to him that in several instances, he'd be forced to raise his voice to make me behave my age, my education, and my humanity as I'd give vent to my ire, my stress, the tension, the fatigue caused by so much bullying of our home, especially of my person, of my womanhood, of being mother and wife. But, my husband never hit me though I was such an insolent, headstrong, impossible woman! He respected me and loved me just the same as when I was close to canonization [teaching in three top schools, one after the other, almost simultaneously, from morning to late evening, with all the driving at the heart and bottlenecks of traffic, advising and mentoring masteral and doctoral students, even the undergraduate English Majors, critiquing their research, theses, and dissertations, checking test papers [all those essays with the local and global errors, really making a lot of blessed among English teachers!]all night long, all year long [!], cleaning and decorating our two modest houses [one in the city, another in the province] non stop for days and weeks, driving for ten to sixteen hours to and fro

Manila and Ilocos every vacation, handwashing mountains of our laundry from 5 p.m. to about 5 a.m. when we had two washing machines but which I sent to our conjugal home in Ilocos, padlocked [!], crazy me!]. His daily routine with our pets, cleaning their cages, walking our dog until she'd had her precious diamonds and had peed, made him a more loving husband and doting father. His demanding and tough routine even became his humor and pleasure especially when each cute feline would do their act of greatness and showcase of feline talent that he'd be calling on us in delight and excitement to witness with him the purring kingdom's acrobats and amazing struts, of course, the lovable tricks of our gentle canine! Oh, he'd give little JP his hot baths every morning [even mine!], clean him up whenever the little angel needed to sit on the toilet, deal patiently with the boy's tantrums and mischief [as the angel loved Mr. Bean a lot!] though with fatherly discipline, and carry him for hours on his arms and shoulders whenever our son was sick or couldn't sleep. He'd watch over me everytime I'd get sick, patiently monitoring overnight my recovery, giving me my meds, feeding, cleaning, and giving me my bath like I were a fragile tender infant! Enzo would never attend to all his work and duty without his Novena to Our Mother of Perpetual Help, with the little Holy Cross safely tucked inside and his Holy Rosary in his pocket. His lips would be full with the little prayers as he'd move here and there to go about his tasks. In the long run, Kitty and her royal court with our Labrador kept my husband faithful to his home and God no matter how much we were bullied, even when the misprision or contempt seemed like pushing us over the cliff of Mt. Precipitation, almost similar to how the hostile, condemning, mocking people of Galilee rejected Jesus Christ because they couldn't believe such a common man is the SAVIOUR OF MANKIND! In our case, because the real unhappy and envious just couldn't accept the joy of our home and simple existence! The Grace of Faith strengthened my husband like the Rock of Gibraltar! Yes, Enzo never forgot to pray, and his unwaivering piety saved him from Satan! My husband came out victorious in the face of great temptation because he was a PRAYERFUL MAN! From the very beginning, from our first date, Enzo had always been genuinely and consistently prayerful. In fact, my anger would many times be quashed by my husband's prayerful ways! Seeing my husband praying fervently the Holy Rosary would stop me from my plot of mischief like my attempt at throwing a dozen of eggs or overriped tomatoes on the enemy! At the peak of unimaginable persecution, my husband wouldn't cease reminding me to forgive and not to become violent while he'd sound very tearful for he must have truly felt my great burden, the enormity of my suffering as I was the main target of all the persecution, all the despiteous, vesicant words! He would talk to me many times to just be more patient with human frailty, with intellectual bedlam and nonsense as well as its prejudice and atrocity, no matter how discordant, delinquent, despicable these can get! He'd remind me of our marriage, our joyful home with our child, of the better things in life, of our blessings, of our plans and dreams, of the great virtues, and of strong faith while he'd do everything he could to protect me and our family from undue persecution instead of resorting to violence. He did his best to shield me, our child, our home from the cruel storms, the grotesque, grisly vicissitudes of life following the words of Jesus. The truly prayerful and meek man in my husband helped him battle and endure the sharp, cutting, piercing blade of atrocity and condemnation. His goodness was like the inextinguishable fire in the coldest and darkest of nights. Indeed, I was very lucky, very fortunate to have been married to such a good man whose heart was so big, so patient, so giving, so loving, so forgiving in spite and despite of all the hostilities, trials, and tough times! Enzo had for most times, exemplified how to be a real, true PEACEMAKER! He struggled with his own temper, his pride, his ego to face human folly fair and square. While at some point he lost his temper from the overwhelming bullying and provocation, he was quick to check himself, and judiciously made amends in all humility and remorse! Mahatma Gandhi's words shone on his ways! He'd forgive the enemies, the persecutors, the oppressors, the bullies for his strength came fom God! My husband's daily routine of feeding and cleaning the cages of our feline and walking our dog or even cleaning Linda Cassiopeia's mess inside the house taught him to be fully and wholly persevering, resilient, and steadfast in the midst of overpowering seemingly insurmountable burden and difficulty. The daily hard labor, the grimy routine served as an unlikely smithy for his steadfast spirit, and forged the greatness of his soul, his faith far from the orchidaceous but the exultation of the Most High! As if my husband offered himself all too willingly and humbly to God the Father in Mt. Gerizim! I'd see him praying a lot his Novena to Our Mother Of Perpetual

Help, praying more intently the Holy Rosary, reading the HOLY SCRIPTURE, praying deeply, patiently, humbly, at times with tears in his eyes and these instances would right away melt my heart, bring me back to my better senses, knocking down my pride, my ivory tower, dissipating or attenuating my erethism, realizing that I am supposed to be the LIGHT OF MY HOME! Yes, the GRACE OF DUTY, OF WORK, OF TASK served its PURPOSE OF PURIFICATION to my husband, to Enzo, A CAGE CLEANER! The sparrows and even the owl can attest to the Magnificent Grace of Human Love, Goodness, and Bursting Faith that championed the man, the husband, the father at the claws of damnation, in the mire of sin! As for our little Joseph, he learned to assist and help his father feed our pets, and clean their cages. He had his cute light blue boots too, and his tiny gloves, and mask. He was learning every move, every gesture, every word and expression of his humble persevering loving father, even how his Papa prayed, and oh, the little boy would even copy then [in his innocence!]how the highly respected language specialist laid in her coffin [for it was his first time to go to a wake and see the dead, and that time, everyone was praying the Holy Rosary! Hence, whenever we'd pray the rosary, he'd instantly lie down, tilt his angelic face a little, cross his little hands, and close his eyes!]. Little JP also learned from his Papa Enzo how to pacify his "rebel" mother by bribing me with body massage and snacks in bed! Indeed, our little zoo, our pets took much of our stress, our pains from the bullying, the persecution, the hostility as we cleaned and fed them. It was Divine Plan that they came to distract us from the evil of human cruelty, from our own personal demons, our unwanted imps and incubi, and to help us focus on our duties and responsibilities as well as to meditate, discern, and pray! Kitty and her throng were sent to us for a great purpose:to remind us of HOW WE SHOULD LIVE in the face of so much adversity, of terrible awful condemnation, persecution, of trying tempting times! Her Royal Highness, her loyal court, and the noble Labrador, Linda Cassiopeia taught us how to pray more fervently, how to be more hopeful in the midst of too much burden and misery; to keep our faith and trust in the words and promises of God, by reading the Holy Bible more often, going to church more regularly, keeping the commandments and the beatitudes in our hearts and souls no matter how much we were tempted to get back at the enemy! Our pets helped us to trust and wait for the fulfilment of God's promise of deliverance from the hands of cruelty; they kept us expectant of the Message of Salvation like when Moses went up to Mt. Sinai to receive the TEN COMMANDMENTS, and Noah's Ark resting on Mt. Ararat where they awaited the rainbow as sign of God's promise for the new life and the end of the great flood! Kitty came in the midst of havoc that midnight of 9 August 2010, which clearly meant she was accompanying us in our journey to Jerusalem, like the lowly but CHOSEN DONKEY, as the dangers [she knew!] were for real and they were many; Kitty fully knew the roads may turn treacherous, destructive, and become infested with the worst of beasts[human insecurities, unfounded fears, periodic angsts, cultural repressions, geographical and psychological displacements, economic oppression, religious persecution, with the self as the most terrifying, much like the fate of the chosen people from the exodus, the long years of suffering, doubt, and despair where many succumbed to the temptations and gave their faith to idols and false gods!], with the legion of the Prince of Darkness or the devil himself! Kitty was the TORCHBEARER as we took that journey, that unknown but beautiful PILGRIMAGE! She took on that important role of assuring us we were taking THE TRAIL, like the prophet Elijah declaring Jesus as the ONE TRUE GOD as he ascended to Mt. Carmel and implored upon God the Father to perform the Miracle of Fire! And her royal court followed to give more help and to provide the little home with a lot more of warmth, of greater joy, of UPLIFTING LOVE to keep us moving to our destination, to make sure we'd reach "THE MANGER!" Linda Cassiopeia likewise served as that BRIGHTEST STAR in the long and difficult journey for the husband and wife to find that warm "MANGER" for their child, making certain that the DESTINED PLACE OF GRACE, THE TRUE OASIS OF DIVINE MERCY would be found despite the perils, in spite of the sins. Our pets kept us faithful and ONE with God! They inspired us to draw strength from the HOLY FAMILY! The daily routine of cleaning our pets' cages, feeding them one by one, walking our Labrador, giving her a bath, removing her lice, bringing those that were too sick to the veterinarians, even in burying those which never recovered, took us away from great and more temptations and sins, distracted us from evil thoughts and plots, miraculously pacified our agitated tormented spirits! Our pets were our angels that protected us from the snares, the machinations, and traps of Lucifer! Each one had a mission to do; to keep the head of the family focused on his duties, on his responsibilities, on the Yoke of Matrimony, on the Yoke of Fatherhood, as well as on the Grace of Faith. To be the unyielding unrelenting pillar of strength, the PERSEVERING LIGHT in the dark as the roads became difficult and dangerous, as THE TRAIL seemed nowhere in sight. Our pets helped my husband to discover more of his hidden unknown inner light, his inward strength, of the true courage of his soul, of his humility and willingness to carry his cross to the Mountain of Skulls or Mt. Calvary, of his submission and obedience to the will of the Father like how Abraham did when God asked him to build that big boat, no matter how much he was being ridiculed, insulted, and mocked, no matter how seemingly senseless, impossible, and harsh life was turning. The daily burdensome routine of being cage cleaners for seven years served as the GRACE OF GRADUAL CONSTANT PURIFICATION, the welcome yet subtle catharsis of the agitated, tormented soul! Indeed, our pets came to deliver us from getting devoured by human weakness, from the encampments of sin, the ugly and terrible sins, outside and in our inner worlds, to help clear the way, show THE TRAIL to the "MANGER!" They gave us the Grace of Silence amidst the billowing cruel waves of persecution! Our pets put us into those precious moments of steadfast reflection, of earnest meditation, of prayerful discernment to ponder and receive the Grace of Wisdom, to welcome the HOLY SPIRIT in our hearts and souls, before the claws of monstrous onerous unbidden adversity. As we took care of them, fed and cleaned them every day, these tasks likewise served to wash away our own pains, our dark thoughts, our sullenness, our share of human folly and sin. Moreover, they paved the way to a lot of priceless, golden moments for us to bond as a loving and caring family in the simple joys of our home, to share and rejoice with the GIFTS OF THE SEASONS OF GRACE [our Christmas Eves, Christmas Days were always so blissfully joyous shared festively, graciously with our big family in Ilocos, our pets full as well with the ABUNDANT GRACE AND PROVIDENCE FROM THE FATHER!]. Truly, our pets helped us find more family time to pray, rejoice, and celebrate in the Wonderful Grace of Unity, of the Grace of Oneness, of the most beautiful GRACE OF ONE LOVE, such precious precious times that will forever bring the sweet smiles and the genuine laughter, wondrous joys and splendid glorious memories that keep the heart beating, whole, and grateful! Our pets taught us in the most trifling yet strangest of ways to face adversity, to bear with burden, misery, and suffering, to persevere with our dreams, to struggle with our sins, to overcome our weaknesses, our vulnerabilities no matter how gargantuan, how distressing, how hard to beat oneself, and likewise, to laugh with our little faults and mistakes, to appreciate EACH MOMENT, to value THE NOW, the Grace of Daily Existence even when the money was scarce or dreams went hiding with the stars. Oh, my husband and son were such a lovable sweet team even when they fought over some spilled cat food as they would then be washing themselves together, eating merrily, and back to their bantering! When one or two feline would try to imitate the overly adventurous Beauty, we'd all just be running to chase, coax, and bring them back to their cages, giving our limbs and muscles time to have mirth in the sun, and the episodes in the volumes of our cheerful verse, to add to the nuclei of the semiotics of rapturous family moments, including saving any of the more sinful ones like Clinton who, after eating his newborn twins by mistake, attempted to hang himself in the big cage but which we were able to foil at dawn for the feline headline news of the day, the riddle of fun and dismay! While our long travels back and forth the city and Ilocos would prove an ordeal to bear and overcome, as we'd thoroughly clean each cage, each feline, and arrange the cages painstakingly in our car or van very early in the morning, then do some spot cleaning under welcoming trees, by some deserted place, even in popular stop overs like the NLEX Shell station, with many eyes curiously watching us, bear the animal natural smell for the eternity of our trips, then feed and clean them right away as we'd reach home or chasing them no end, injuring our knees, bruising our hands, all these just made us even closer, supportive, and more united as a family. The cumbrousness of the routine and the epic labor of both body and mind just tied us together no matter the kaon or the massive force that wanted to tear us apart and scatter our souls to Erebus! Oh, our little zoo gave us the best of Hemera upon the weight of the Cross for the LOVE OF GOD never fails to replenish and sustain the vitality of human faith! Our pets led us to some strange but beautiful world...they took us to "THE TRAIL"... leading in a "Manger," with the child, with the animals! Our little JP came not so much with grand attention but in a uniquely austere, quiet, but perfectly special way, unlike any other, completing our joy, our home! He grew up day by day with the routine of our ordinary simple family life. And what was very unusual of our little son while we lived in that "destined place", and up to this day has always been his genuine love for animals especially dogs and cats and vice versa! They would just follow him so meekly and willingly whenever he'd walk the streets or when we'd go to the public market where stray cats and tamed dogs would just suddenly come to our son. JP is truly heaven's answer to our prayers, a sweet mischievous loving cherub, a truly favoured little child of God! Indeed, those seven years gave us the most precious GIFTS OF THE MANGER that kept our home joyful, hopeful, and faithful despite the dangers, the temptations, the sins. But to recount in greater detail my own difficult personal purification or my journey in PURIFYING PERSECUTION, I'd whisper on Kitty to show me once more THE TRAIL as mine would see me carry my cross in more tears, greater pains, undesired infinite sins, though my soul knows with special blessing...IN THE GRACE OF PENITENCE. I shall open my heart more to you in the next and last chapter...

## Chapter Five

## Roads to Jerusalem and the Black Serpent: To Love With the Birds

I WIPE HIS FACE WITH my crumpled pink hanky as my tears keep falling, my hands trembling, my heart…gone…My beloved is dead. It is one twenty-eight in the morning of April 11, 2017. My Enzo, in medical parlance, has expired, has left me and our child…including our extended family, our menagerie…our home…our dreams, our future…the sharpest dagger of woe and sorrow is deep within my heart, the heart that used to be perfectly happy, the heart that loved SUCH A MAN…yes, my heart is gone…this fateful dawn of holy Tuesday! O, WHAT PAIN IS GREATER THAN THIS…O, WHAT CURSE IS WORST TO KISS THE LIFELESS LIPS OF ONE'S ETERNITY? LOVE IS CLEAVED, TORN, AND BROKEN INTO SMITHEREENS OF PUNISHING REMORSE AND REGRET FOR EVERY MOMENT THEN THROWN TO RANCOR AND CONCEIT!

"Ma'am please, let us clean Sir…" The teary-eyed gentle-faced male nurse almost whispers as he tries to take me away from the ICU bed of my dead husband. Yes, Enzo is dead. He is dead. My Adonis caring, gentle, loving husband is dead. Today, Tuesday of the Holy Week is eight days away from our 13th civil wedding anniversary, and almost a month away from our 13th church wedding anniversary. Almost twenty-five years of loving each other…what satire, what satire of the ad infinitum of our LOVE'S INFINITY!

I touch his hair, his thick black wavy hair with the handsome gray; my tears become a dangerous river. I shout and curse and scream. The ICU is bare with anything but life's worst moments! The world has totally stopped. There's nothing that can thwart the painful truth. Not a single rose could bear the heart's sorrow! The ICU is totally quiet while the well-loved spoiled wife wails in the deepest of the deepest of the most excruciating, searing, most punishing pain. She is now the widow of that UP Diliman professor who smiled so handsomely and enigmatically at her in Rm. 320 of the College of Education in April 1992…in 1984…

"Mama, here's your tea. Drink it while it's hot. Here, I got you *ensaymada*, your favorite!" Enzo, my husband never fails to treat me his special cosmopolitan tea[Lipton tea with Nido milk and his Splenda], morning, afternoon, and midnight plus of course his surprise pastries and delicacies that he hides in his now worn out blue Jansport knapsack because the little angel might devour them all in a split second. We have our best bondings, our simple but precious little "conjugal, marital dates" at midnight or even the wee hours while our cherub is fast asleep. *"Ano nga pala* Filipino for frozen, liquid, and solid assets?" I ask him and we laugh so hard while he gives me the witty translations. JP moves a little on his bed so we both cover our mouths full of the *ensaymada*, the linguistics, and the laughter. For almost thirteen years of our married life, it has been Language Teaching[SLA, ESL, EFL]that would serve as our bread and butter as well as our leisure, pleasure, and also, pressure! In fact, all our lives! We'd exchange notes, talk of our classes, fun class moments and the torture as well as humor of laidback scholarship, share anecdotes on the more colorful students and mentees[with me ending up so pissed off when my husband starts to mention female names!]. Indeed, linguistics has made our marriage stable and yet, "troublesome" with all those fan clubs of Enzo! One very obsessed female admirer even undressed and exhibited her totally nude human anatomy to my husband in his much younger years that he ran out of his office like an Olympian! Since my husband was an exceptionally good and fun SLA speaker, even the National Bilibid Prison invited him on their Graduation Commencement Exercises, with all the prison guards, the warden, and the prisoners holding their tummies from laughter as Professor Enzo Quiambao Quiambao talked of sociolinguistics in action! How I'd exploit [oh, lovingly!] my husband's brilliance and kindness that I'd ask him to lecture on ESL or EFL, anthropological linguistics or historical linguistics, all the seven branches on the spot, whether he'd be in the shower, on our bed[oh, even when we were making love!], frying my favorite snacks, *kwek kwek,* feeding the pets or cleaning their cages, or while we'd be driving from UP to UST, many times of this when I've forgotten the theories or when I've failed to read my books, oh, his books! Our books, yes, would make us fight one day, then fight another day when we both could not find them! And the culprit? Me! I'd lend my husband's precious books to my undergraduate and graduate students, then I'd forget, and many of these print gems would be lost or missing, that Enzo would soon be shedding his tears while I'd be lashing on him why his books are missing! Yes, our married life would see us bantering non-stop with our own brands and versions of linguistics until I'd fart so loud that Enzo would almost die from too much laughing while our cups of cosmopolitan tea would then be cold or empty, and likewise, we'd then be fighting because of the yellow-eyed monster or my PMS then much later, my menopause! But my husband would never ever hurt me as he'd remain very faithful even until that moment, those moments in the ICU.

They run! Oh God, the doctors are all running to that curtained cubicle! I fall with my ocean of tears on the very cold and hard floor. The hospital security surround me. Their tears fall for the woman lying and wailing and screaming on the sympathetic dirty white. My husband just went flatline! My heart has not known of such intense pain! My sister's death in 2005 had pierced my heart but the years seemed to have healed the wound though the scar has remained. And now, it's my husband! The doctors are many and they act so fast and then stop. The louder I cry. "Ma'am, *halika na po...*Sir is revived! He's got a heartbeat!" The women security hush hush me and bring me up to my feet. They let me sit on the sofa. My nephew, Aries Christian strokes my back and gives me a cold bottle of mineral water. His face is sullen with tears. He knows how much I love his *Tito* Enzo. His *Tita* Millie waited twelve long years for THE ONLY MAN in her life for them to finally be able to get married in church and in the city hall! Oh, the doctors are all running again! Towards that cubicle! This time it takes them twenty minutes to revive my husband! I fall back on the floor, and I wail with my unknown fury, cursing fate, cursing the world! The security try hard to carry me to the sofa but to no avail as I kick them here and I kick them there! I am but the most dreadful of wild horses! But they are very patient, very understanding, very compassionate. My rage and my pain are more than what Mt. Vesuvius could ever unleash! My heart is gone while my soul is as wretched as the eternally damned! I have become a living dead! Today is Palm Sunday, April 9, 2017. WHAT TERROR, WHAT BEAST COMETH TO GRIP IN THE NECK THE SAINT THAT BROUGHT HEAVEN TO EARTH! OH, IS THERE NO MARTYRDOM WITH TEARS SPARED FOR THE HEART? WHY STEAL LOVE'S PROMISES WITH THE BLOOD OF SAINT? CRUEL WINGS OF DEATH!

"Ma'am, let us assist you, please! You cannot do it yourself. We need the help of the surgical team...they'll take care of Sir's tubes. Please *po* Ma'am!" The male nurse takes me to the other side of the ICU bed. My husband lies so handsome but lifeless. They slowly but efficiently remove each of those tubes from his mouth, his nose, his neck, his body. Then, they are finished. I continue to clean my beloved Enzo while my tears fall on Frost's desert places...

His face looks very peaceful. There seems to be a quick sweet smile as I clean the blood from his mouth. His eyebrows are still those heavenly bushes. The big mole on his left eyebrow still feels nice. I gently close his eyes with my now more steady fingers though my tears flow deep to the catacombs of lost love, of lost Eden! His long thick eyelashes keep very still. When did I last see those perfect eyes look at me so lovingly?

"Oh my God! He just opened his eyes! Papa, Papa I love you soooo much!!! Nurse, nurse, please call the doctors!" I'm so overjoyed that I'm jumping like a child at the ICU. My husband just gave me his most loving glance! I saw once more those almost gray, most beautiful eyes of a man, of the only man I've ever loved, and the only man who truly loved and respected me! For a second...then he closed them...forever...This day was 10 April 2017, my father's 84th birthday. Nothing compares to the pain of closing the eyes of your dead loved one...the first, with my dear sister, *Manang* Erleen, and now, my beloved husband...cruel, cruel pain!

O ESPERANCE, WHY DEPART THY SWEET PROMISE OF AN ETERNITY OF BLISS! SUCH EXULTATION OF TRUE LOVE'S KISS ---STOLEN IN THE FLIGHT OF BIRDS AND THE PAVID WHISPERS AMONGST NO SAINTS!

"Ma'am, let's bring Sir down *na po*...Please *po* Ma'am! The longer he stays here, *mas lalaki po ang babayaran natin...*" The same male nurse tries to cover my husband with a white blanket.

"No, you're not taking him anywhere! Don't you cover him with that cloth! Stay away!" I hold the cold toes of my Enzo. I kiss his hands. I hug him tight. I cry again. WHAT BEATS THE SORDID TRUTH OF SLUGGISH BEAST UPON THE THRONE OF LIFE? NOTHING CAN HOARD MY PAIN BUT THE SWELLING VENGEANCE OF TOMORROW AND THE SNEERS OF EMPTY DREAMS!

## THE HANDS OF JOB, THE HANDS OF LOVE

"Emy, *andito na ako!* I love you!" He kisses my forehead and my cheeks. Enzo is wearing the first jacket I've given him on his 46th birthday, August 10, 1993. He touches and caresses my hair, my head, and hugs me. It's around four in the morning. He just came from Manila, I just got out of St. James Hospital in Vigan after my almost three week confinement from my first major surgery, *Volvulus with Secondary Malrotation.* I was born with floating intestines [oh, actually, with a lot of factory defect!], and they suddenly got paralyzed, I almost died if not for my surgeon, Dr. James Alday, who just got back to the Philippines from his thirty-three years of medical practice at the John Hopkins Hospital, U. S. A.,[if I remember it right.]. "Honeybabe, *ikaw na ba iyan?*" I whisper as I'm still high with my painkillers. Enzo had to leave for Manila the third day I was confined, and after my surgery to raise money for my hospital bills. He's back with almost a hundred thousand to settle the amount. Today is my birthday, November 18, 1996.

"Emy, honeybabe, take this, your antibiotic." My boyfriend sits me up on my hospital bed in New World City. I got chicken pox all over. Enzo then combs my hair, and continues spoonfeeding me with the hot *molo* soup, afterwhich he slices the red apple for my dessert. This year is around 1999. He and *Manang* Erleen take turns in looking after me at the hospital as he has daily classes in UP. My beautiful sister buys me my delicate dainties as usual. Enzo then pays for my hospital bill, and brings me home to my Kalayaan apartment, in Quezon City where every night, there's always the queer sound of foosteps going down the staircase. My boyfriend would visit me every day, every night and drives back home to his UP Diliman housing unit blowing his horns three times the moment he exited from our building's parking lot. How the security guards were "entertained" or intrigued and oh, got so amused by the blowing horns and the romantic lover!

"Mama, how are you feeling?" My husband just got back from UP to file for his GSIS loan. I am in the hospital again. It's 2007. I am scheduled for a major surgery[my second!] as they found a big cyst in my left ovary[Thank God, it's benign!], and my intestines are sour floating once more! They got loose after almost eleven years. My surgeon is the huge but excellent Dr. Tuazon, who'd check for himself where my heart really is as the much younger medical interns have two opposing diagnoses; one, my heart beats on the right, the other, my heart palpitates on the left. I've always thought my heart was on trees and with my little pen, of course, the best part with my husband! On the day before my surgery, I begin to talk odd; I'd recite endless poetry, especially Wordsworth's, Robert Burns's, and the sonnets of Shakespeare["...oh she walks in beauty and delight!" I'd say this line repeatedly to my obygyne, Dra. Navarro, look alike of Jamie Lee Curtis, who'd strut in and out of my hospital room in fabulous, real classy skirts!], and talk to everyone just in English, sounding of the Philippines'inner circle of Dr. Martin's[Can you believe that!], that some young nursing students would hesitate to come inside my room, the English speaking patient's room! Maybe because at this time, I concurrently sit as Chair and Coordinator of the General Education Department and English Area of Assumption College, San Enzo, Makati, a top exclusive school for girls from the high end like Forbes Park that perhaps my tongue got so acculturated or ambitiously assimilated, my *social climbing-langue accent*! After my surgery, I'm still on the *Englisera* mood, but now it's turned into Hollywood variety, and every doctor who comes inside my room is a Hollywood star, sending all those proud smiles and little good laughs on the faces, mouths, and dangling flattered stethoscopes of both obviously elated male and female doctors that they'd say, I was their favorite patient ever!

The most hilarious? I saw SUPERMAN right after I opened my eyes at the recovery room, with me shouting in all awe and unbelieving astonishment, "Oh, it's a bird it's a plane, it's Dr. Superman! The young doctor was so red, blushing all over while everyone applauded and cheered in *gusto* and pleasant tolerance of my *highs* from the mischievous anesthesia! My young male doctor really looked like Christopher Reeve, that one *doktora,* young, pimpled, and sweet expressed so much regret for not getting him in a *shotgun marriage*! Well, she sounded joking but her eyes spoke the truth. But life has its bad jokes, *palabiro ang tadhana.* That hospital was where my husband would then die, ten years later, and where I'd then be driving fast and furious into their front- glassed lobby, stop with my screeching tires right there at the entrance with my hazard lights on, and cry in my lone dauntless voice my fight for justice for my husband who was glaringly killed from medical malpractice, holding on my left his favorite shirt while on my right his favorite polo *barong*, with my fiery graffiti; my little son crying hungry and fatherless inside Silver Angel, our Avanza van.

## THE AGONIZING ROADS TO JERUSALEM

It's almost four in the morning. Tuesday, Holy Week. I'm holding the big once dutiful, caring, and loving hands of my dead husband. We are passing through the hospital corridors to the elevator. People try to avoid us, and they run away, just like how those others did when we were taking *Manang* Erleen to that freezer! My heart is stabbed seven times seven, a countless times! We are taking my beloved to the Morgue at the basement. When did JP and I find ourselves going to that morgue? That was a week before Enzo had his TRANSURETHRAL RESECTIONING OF THE PROSTATE SURGERY or TURP which led to his massive bleeding and heart attack that killed him! We went to buy midnight snacks as my husband was also starved, then we got lost to find ourselves later proceeding to the hospital morgue. JP was shaking hard then from fear and fright. Enzo had that sad look in his face as he was listening to our frightful midnight adventure. My heart would not bother to entertain that odd feeling that crept in, dismissing it right away, just like the odd times I'd see death in his face[!] even years before, or that moment I discovered of the headless groom-figurine in 2005!

The room is freezing cold. They transfer him on that very cold stainless steel. I remember how he'd proudly tell the good priests, our friends that he drives his stainless owner jeep back and forth and around UP almost every day. Oh, how destiny casts its woeful and most cruel glare. I tell the nurses I'm staying inside and they simultaneously exclaim, "Oh no, Ma'am! You can't stay here inside!" Hence, I sit outside that freezing cold room like a stone sentinel, my numbness crawling fast, I do not feel. EXCEPT that I now see the woman who kissed the forehead of my husband as he lay critical in Rm. 505. My teeth gnashed like the beasts in the wilds, and my fingers turned into claws, my eyes burned! How the sword's blade wanted to smite Shakespeare's TRAITOR! Oh such cruel pain leaves the soul not a shred of sanity! The claws of vengeance ready for the strike! But my brother was seated beside me, and he clipped my claws with his tearful face. Then my dear old friend, Fr. Bien MiguelB came to bless my dead husband while he was lying in the morgue, with that bright yellow liquid coming out of his nose, this painful episode I had witnessed with my dead mother's in 1972. An agonizing déjà vu!

From the Morgue of the big hospital to St. Peter Chapels, Quezon Avenue, I find no elegy to ease my pain, none whatsoever brings the prayer to my lips. My eyes blur with tears as the ambulance speeds far from that place of my eternal woes. BUT TODAY IS NO YESTERDAY WHEREUPON THE VERSE FEARS NOT THE SHADOW OF FIFTEEN GHOSTS, NOW MARCHING IN THE GRANDIOSE STRIDES ON THE HORIZON, LEAVING THE FILTH IN THE MEMORY OF SEAGULLS BUT THE RIDDLE OF THE SPHINX, THE PHOENIX SHALL EMBLAZON WITH THE BLOOD OF SAINT!

From St. Peter Chapels to the first autopsy of my husband, I get into the classic murder scene of the Roman Czar, Julius Caesar! My soul is lost in hell! HOW SWIFT ARE THE WINGS OF TIME, LEAVING NOT A TEAR IN THE POTICHE OF ANGELS BUT IN THE SMEAR OF FATE, O THE SCOUNDREL HAS SLIVERED MARY'S HEART, WOE TO ME WHEREAS TIME CAME TO DRINK UPON THAT SPRING OF GREAT LOVE BUT TREASURED NOT THE MOMENT!

THE WHITE COFFIN, REMORSE AND REGRET. Was it not

only on 14 February 2017 that he handed me a single stem of red rose and some local chocolates while he walked towards me and our little JP to help me with my bag and books from my UST BS BIOLOGY class, with whom I passionately taught the constructs of thesis, anti-thesis, and synthesis, and the future young doctors commenting their English professor was kind of unorthodox not talking of rules and requirements on first day of class but of the riddles of life? I forgot it was Valentine's Day! My class, my chores, and my menopause occupied my consciousness that I forgot to even write a sweet note for my very patient and loving husband! I didn't know that was the last valentine I'd be celebrating with him. And, never did I suspect that was THE LAST ROSE FOR MILLIE…

There are so many. Some are brown, gold, and silver with price tags! I keep walking inside that large basement, where in a corner, my husband is lying very quiet and still. Then I see the white casket. My tears are back and they fall like blood. I mumble to the man close by that noble white is fitting and right for my Enzo. My tears come now as the Nile, ancient mystic but forever flowing and deep. My remorse is great, I clutch the HOLY ROSARY. I try to pray while they carry my beloved to his eternal bed. His UP *Sablay* falls and they put it back. I sob louder now as I remember how I'd lash out on my husband when he'd be reading his little books while slicing the onions, the garlic, and the overriped tomatoes; how I'd easily forget in years that I was married to a dedicated teacher, a true scholar, a humble intellectual. My guilt is the Sahara, scorching, oh, enormously scorching; my knees weaken and I embrace the white coffin. I cry to the Blessed Mother to intercede for my intense pain. I stand beside her weeping before the cross. My husband's white coffin sees me back into the road of salvation. Emily Dickinson's "Solemnest of Industries" echoes, and I battle with the devil to give my husband his decent wake though I'd then reprimand the female make up artist of the funeral home to change the pink lipstick of my husband into pale brown!

Early morning, April 12, 2017. Fifteen Minutes Of AGONY IN THE GARDEN.

The stretch from St. Peter's to UP Diliman seemed an eternity of unspeakable pain! I was taking my husband to the university he loved so much, the university he served with utmost dedication and selfless service for thirty-seven years. Quezon Avenue looked like a deserted winding road in some forgotten city; the dim lights melancholic, the trees like remorseful begging souls. The early breeze was haunting, and my tears all the more punishing, punitory to the memory...punitive to my lyric of once great pure love. My ten year-old is sleepy and quiet, too quiet, while Judith, my much younger cousin fixes her flaming orange scarf and shawl as she utters dismay for the recklessness of the funeral home's ahead of us with the unaffected flamboyance of her long curly burgundy hair, matching perfectly her magenta lipstick. I try to drive in the frenzy of my emotions and the stirring vehemence of my thoughts. Once we reached the famous UP OBLATION, the nude and proud symbol of the country's best minds through the decades, the funeral car just went speeding like the sleek French bullet train along sprouting and blossoming dozens and dozens of sunflowers, their plant ancestry from the equally famous, UPLB which trained a number of Vietnamese scholars how to plant and harvest good rice that now, they also export the good rice to the Philippines. Oh, the funeral car goes here, goes there, goes everywhere, all around the University of the Philippines vast and sprawling campus where all the trees are waving their giant boughs and *esprit de corps* to the well-loved, highly respected professor, ever so handsome and dashing in his *Barong Tagalog* inside that white coffin that would then glisten so esoterically beautiful under the fading moonlight and the breaking of a new day as the dutiful and able busy hands carried his casket to the Mortuary of the state university he loved with all loyalty, conviction, and philanthropy. My heart mourns and grieves in the agonizing sorrow of the GARDENS OF THE CHURCH OF THE HOLY SACRIFICE, seemingly putting me in that GARDEN OF GETHSEMANE, beside my God, My Saviour, my Jesus Crucified in Mount Calvary. My lips have began to recite again the Lord's Prayer and the Blessed Mother's. The devil scowls and leaves in no time.

THE WAKE IN THE CITY. Then, they came. My dead husband's first guests. The noble throng of feline. With a woman, the Good Samaritan.

They came to his wake like a mourning march that Holy Wednesday morning, while the sun was making its tempered ascent and climb. The sky was bluish and tearful but the fowls of the air sang on gracious yet melancholic branches and even atop the grief of the cold black room where a large HOLY CROSS with a blood-covered Jesus hung, His loving eyes cast down on dead Enzo in his white casket. Yes, the birds were singing as the noble throng came and walked in the mortuary one by one, in prayerful silence. They went around the white coffin slowly, carefully, in reverence of a GOOD MASTER. They sat in corners, while one or two came to kiss the little child's innocent but fagged out shoes. Then, the largest and seemingly oldest of them approached me and purred like she was saying her deepest sympathies and heartfelt condolences. Oh, her tummy was bulging with life, and later that morning, she gave birth to three beautiful kittens right on the ledges of the dreariness and drab of the black-railed room where the once well-loved and all too pampered mother and child cry their silent tears on the cold and dusty wooden benches and rely on the magnanimous compassion, help, and wit of the young doctor of literature who has been up and awake and busy all night long with her well-poised stilettoes, talking domineeringly confident and polite with the funeral home's personnel, her student-leaders, her friends, colleagues, and relatives, with her long curly burgundy hair so elegantly propped up and ready to welcome and receive the sympathies and condolences of both the feline kingdom and humanity. After a peaceful eternity of feline homage and last respects for the good Master, the throng leaves in the solemnity of the holy place, of the sacred grounds…but posting three of them in corners of the very quiet room which included the most elderly and pregnant feline, with the candles glowing in the faint ray of the morning sun.

Then she comes, The Good Samaritan Woman.

She is in shabby beggar's clothes. Her name is of Eve, and she smiles with her broken teeth. She walks in and asks who is the UP professor in the coffin. Then she wipes her tears with her dirty hands as she says, *"Kaibigan ko po si Sir Quiambao, matagal na. Napakabuti niya! Palagi niya akong inaabutan!"* [Sir Quiambao has been my good friend for more than three decades. He was A GOOD MAN. Always with coins or twenty peso-bills for me in his pocket.]. Then she blows her nose this time with the sleeves of her old and torn blouse. I offer her my pink hanky but give her what's left of my cousin's tissue instead as I'd then recall that pink was my most sorrowful in the terror of loss on that Holy Tuesday "breaking dawn" of 11 April 2017. The woman comforts and consoles me and my child with more of her fond and fun memories and anecdotes of the UP professor who was kind and fair to everyone, with his incomparably fluent and politely eloquent *Bulakeno Tagalog*, embellishing and enriching a more exuberantly impassioned nationalistic FILIPINO that he excitedly, proudly, and excellently taught in the classrooms of UP Diliman with the *iskolars ng bayan*, the Japanese, the Chinese, the Thai, and the Koreans, and all over the Philippines, and as far as the world's number one economic superpower, the United States of America. The good Samaritan woman then said her good-byes and last respects to her humble, respectable intellectual good friend of about thirty-three years as she did all the dirty work in the university campus. I felt so comforted by the good woman of Jesus of Nazareth.

Before that first day of my husband's wake in the UP Mortuary ended, with me falling in deep, very DEEP SLEEP for the first time in my life [maybe God's way of consoling me for the terrible misery and to prepare me for more sorrows to come], my worn out silently grieving purple shoes on my feet, tears dried up in my eyes, my little son snoring in his fatigue of carrying his mother at least to the edge of her kingsize matrimonial bed, the good loving Thomasians came in full force, including colleagues and friends from the UST community. They came early in pairs, in groups. They loved my husband though he never taught in UST; almost then, in the seasons that were to come as we both were requested by the Dean of the UST Graduate School to design the UST TESOL Program of the university. My husband's book on SLA theories and principles, published by the UP OPEN UNIVERSITY has likewise been used as reference by my graduate classes through the years. The Thomasians pooled their resources together to buy food and drinks for the sympathetic guests, and flowers, and mass cards, and candles for their Sir Enzo who'd welcome them so warmly and graciously in our humble UP Diliman home, sharing selflessly and humbly with them his expertise in SLA. The good priests also came in the evening[Fr. Bienvenido Miguel, with his kind foreigner friend, also a priest though I failed to meet them and attend their concelebrated mass as JP and I were sent home by the concerned and thoughtful UP alumni to rest and take a bath!], and the following morning of Maundy Thursday, our dear Fr. Ubaldus Djonda, SVD delivered a most heart-rending yet so inspiring, comforting, consoling, and uplifting homily, with his Thomasian classmates assisting[my dear Danny Balanse and sweet Abigail Patrice Sibug; the ever helpful Ramil Pellogo was out of town then.] and singing during the liturgy with the loving and compassionate Rooseveltians who, just like the Thomasians, came with their tearful eyes and genuine sympathies even on the very first hours of their Sir Enzo's wake, handing to me their hard-earned pennies out of their deep love and gratitude to that noble professor who inspired and taught them so excellently and treated them very well in spite of their own shortcomings as students. The maroons came by batches[politicians, bankers, scientists, lawyers, marketing executives, realtors, educators, doctors], with their recollections and reminiscences of their *GURO*[since their UP Elementary, UPIS, UPD days], as well as their generous sincere help and donations. Yes, everyone who loved my husband came to pay him their last respects. On those two days, the rest of the alumni, colleagues, friends, and students came to say kind words, beautiful tales and infinite odes of admiration for the good professor in the white coffin, *ANG DAKILANG GURO NG FILIPINO AT PINOY LINGGWISTIKA NG UNIBERSIDAD NG PILIPINAS SA DILIMAN NG TATLONG DEKADA.*

## THE LONGEST HOURS, THE TORTUOUS SORROWFUL ROAD TO JERUSALEM

It's GOOD FRIDAY, April 14, 2017. I am travelling early morning today with my little son and my dead husband. Widow and orphan in their Silver Angel Avanza, driven by a quiet compassionate bald St. Peter's, and the loving Man Of The House, in the L300…the noble white coffin sealed for the long road travel…the journey home…the most painful journey to our home…A WIDOW'S CARRYING OF THE CROSS…

"Mama, please defensive driving *lang!* Here's your sugarfree candy." My husband Enzo reminds me gently to be careful and easy with the accelerator as we traverse the North Luzon Expressway[NLEX]. We are again bound to Ilocos Sur for our Christmas vacation, and as usual, overloaded with the big family Christmas gifts, the new pairs of sneakers and *polos* for father and son, the blouses and slacks for the mother-lady driver, and the meds for the little zoo! JP is safely tucked and buckled up at the back with his bundle of all the world's junk[courtesy of his crazy Mama Millie to keep him still and peaceful! One time, I bought little JP the largest popcorn that he ended up in the hospital I couldn't forgive myself then!]. Beside our son is Linda Cassiopeia who's joyfully admiring the green scenery and great history of every town, of every province. Behind our Labrador are the colourful cages of the sleepy feline browns, blacks, and whites who purr softly in languid for they know they'd just get their rations in the Ilocandia kingdom, and that means, after twelve to thirteen hours, or sometimes 16 hours[!] when the humans want to linger much longer in the gasoline stations, their toilets, and their delicacies. Especially with the Hot Bowls Of Soup!

"Mama, I got you Beef Wanton!" Enzo excitedly spoonfeeds me the hot noodle soup with the fresh lettuce. Chowking is always divine whenever we travel as well as the rest of local restaurants and the eateries serving all kinds of hot soup, very good especially for my tummy and capriciously desultory intestines. "My God, Papa, this is wonderful!" I'd always repeatedly exclaim for every hot bowl my sweet thoughtful caring husband would get from those heavenly kitchens and diners and *kainans* along the almost four hundred kilometre stretch, passing by five big provinces from Metro Manila[Bulacan, Pampanga, Tarlac, Pangasinan, and La Union], each with its own unique culture, brave heroes, and good people until my homeprovince, Ilocos Sur, of course, the home of the great hardworking thrifty pious and ambitious Ilocanos! Enzo is as pleased and happy as ever whenever he hears of my compliments of those hot bowls with the *molo, arroz caldo, luglug, chicken mami,* of course, the beef wanton, the *lugaw,* and my favorite, the *goto*[rice porridge with pig intestines and the earth's greens!].

NLEX, 3 a.m. The L300 is fast but my eyes won't let go of its tail lights. The *Agoho* trees are ghosts of woe; I weep. WHILST THE AIR BREATHES TO MAKE THOSE LEAVES FLUTTER, MY SORROW PITHS ME, THROWS ME TO WHERE DEATH CANS'T EVEN BEAR TO HOLD A SINGLE TEAR!

We speed through the winding expressway until Meycauayan, Bulacan. I wail in the holocaust of smouldering pain! The man in the UP *Sablay* says good-bye to his hometown, his birthplace.

"Emy, this is Malhacan, Meycauayan. I was born and raised here by my parents." My boyfriend of two days excitedly tells me as we drive through a handsome town of a few factories, big and small houses, old and new, with people smiling, cordial, and warm. Today is September 12,

1992. It's our first visit to Enzo's family. Joseph, his youngest brother is shy and reserved while Gie, his wife is bubbly and warm. Enzo introduces me to his younger sister, Zeny married to a Puno. She smiles and offers me something to eat. Gie brings the soda and other Bulacan delicacies. I am 29, very shy, and so in love! Enzo then drives us to his other younger brother's[Danny] house in Malolos, Bulacan. But *kuya* Danny isn't there as he works in Japan[for the *lapad* or precious yen to send his kids to school!] but then would later gift me with nice white curtains for my windows in my Kalayaan unit. *Aling Matti*, his seamstress wife cooks her specialty dish of quail egg-stuffed giant fresh squid. My dear God, the best ever! But I shouldn't eat much[though I could eat the entire squid kingdom in that perfect cuisine!]as it's Filipino custom to be not so *matakaw*[gluttonous!] on the first visit of a boyfriend's house or his relative's. *"Sayang!"* I murmur to my appetite as I smile sweetly to the gracious and hospitable charming though serious-looking woman. My boyfriend then gives me a tour of all other towns. Bustos, Bulacan would then become witness to many of our honeymoon days in the sun while Meycauayan is forever the historic hometown of a legend, The Legend Of A Farmer Who Went To UP and The University Of Washington With His Thick Wavy Hair and His *bugtongs* or riddles. For didn't he excitedly tell his *Tatang* Berto one day they were ploughing the farm that he'd be riding that big jetplane someday as it flew over their handsome heads? And he did, with the world's top lecturing grant, no less than Fulbright!

It's around 4 a.m. Bamban Bridge, Pampanga.

"Yehey! The bridge of our dreams! Vacation time again!" All three[father, mother, and child!] shout in glee. Bamban Bridge has become a herald of our family fun-filled land travels to Ilocos and definitely, our wonderful joyful home vacations. Enzo and I started building in early 2000 our conjugal house even when we were still to be married in early 2005. But now, the melange of curses for love thrown by wastrels who dwell in the gutters of the glutton among rodents! WHERE ARE YOU BELLEROPHON? WHY HAVE YOU NOT STRUCK ME? AM I NOT CHIMERA? THIS PAIN IS UNBEARABLE! DID I NOT THROW THAT WEDDING RING IN THE TOILET OF THAT HOSPITAL WHERE MY BELOVED MADE HIS LAST? YES, I AM CHIMERA! STRIKE ME AS I DO NOT DESERVE A SECOND TO LIVE!!!

The L300 comes to a full stop. Our driver pulls over too. Tarlac. Both drivers politely ask us to take breakfast with them. JP is still drowsy. I shake my head, the little boy too. The men proceed to the eatery for bowls of hot soup. I choke as my child and I stare at the quiet L300 parked beside us. O WHO COULD TAKE THIS CUP OF SORROW BUT THE FAREWELL OF MEMORY WHILST AUTUMN'S SUNSETS SKETCH IN THE INNOCENCE OF LAMBS!

Rosales, Pangasinan. 2003. "Honeybabe, *ingat!*" Enzo reminds me as I run to SM Rosales to get him my Christmas gift, a Dickies Polo, the first of his a dozen before three year-old JP would set most of them on fire inside the cabinet of his Papa one day he finds Mr. Bean so funny, burning an entire house! I got him a light pink and yellow and green checkered short-sleeved polo that he'd wear years later on that fateful day of 28 March 2017, with my Enzo WALKING SO SPIRITEDLY, SO ENERGETICALLY, VERY MUCH ALIVE, FULL OF LIFE, HOPE, AND DREAMS! No sonnet of Shakespeare can quash or dissipate the maddening pain and anger in my heart! None of the most tragic of tragedies could ever compare to the INCUBUS OF MEDICAL MALPRACTICE! O, if there's any of those vultures to feast on my pain, on my torture, on my torment, on my sorrow! O, destiny too ugly and cruel! IF ONLY EDGAR ALLAN POE KNEW ME THEN, HE COULD HAVE JUST THROWN ME OFF THAT DEEPEST RAVINE ON THE COLDEST DARKEST NIGHT OF UNCARING AUTUMN WITH THE SHARPEST DAGGER RIGHT AT THE MIDDLE OF MY HEART! THIS PAIN SHOULDN'T HAVE COME BY SUMMER'S DAYLIGHT!

Urdaneta, Pangasinan. The best French fries! "Mama, I'll just run to the Rest Room!" My husband takes advantage of the long line of cars on the Drive Thru of Kentucky. I make our usual orders and never without the biggest and most tasteful fries! It's always the yummy Kentucky chicken, mashed potato, coleslaw salad, and mushroom soup that signal it's lunch time of our long but joyful travel, either to Ilocos or back to Manila. While in the hospital that mournful year of 2017, I'd manage to snatch some time to the Burger King drive thru along Timog to get my husband and son burgers and fries very late at night after I've fed our pets and have cleaned their cages as fast as a wink. The white gentle Snowy would then die while my husband was brain dead in the ICU. Maybe to sit on some fragrant path as the feline awaits the Good Master...

Shell Station, Sison, La Union. "Mama, let me check if they still have *ensaymada*. I'll get you your next cup of brewed coffee!" Enzo and JP would then proceed to the Shell store of delicacies, good affordable coffee, and the rest of their best offers to land travellers. Curious eyes would focus either on the bumper of our Silver Angel with the sticker, PROUD TO BE UP!, or at the driver's door, with HARVARD UNIVERSITY sticker, and still, on the front passenger door, University of the Philippines. My husband's joy was so overwhelming and overflowing upon his retirement in 2013 that he almost filled our newly bought Avanza with every sticker he got in his cabinet! The little tale of the Harvard U. sticker comes with fondness and regret. The sticker was given by Enzo's American student at the University of Washington who just transferred from the world-famous number one Ivy League university of the U.S., and where I was to go in 2006 for a Fulbright research grant, fearlessly and fiercely competed with one or two other short listers, but alas, I didn't get it for not having taught yet creative writing. The rest, well, is some history, at least for me, an unknown struggling Filipino author.

Every town of La Union was memorized by my husband, who, at the time of his death, 69 years old, still had a photographic memory, what with all the peanuts he had eaten since he was a child plus all the hard-boiled eggs as he'd jokingly tell me. Even if it was just his first class meeting to some twenty or fifty students, he'd remember at once their names a hundred per cent! My memory would always be a far cry from his that while I'd be holding the seatplan of my class, I'd rumble my students' names especially the undergrad that the'y laugh their hearts out every now and then except when my coordinator sat at the back to observe, the sweet millennials conspired with their English Professor to be christened, each with a new name! Of course, I gave them all their passing grades! How my husband laughed that bonding midnight I told him of my class tale for the day.

AGOO. Another memorable town. They have one of the biggest Catholic churches in the North, and how the more beautiful it is every Christmas season as the town always adorns their church with ingenious local art and craft aside from the numerous lights, making the historic church so inviting of every sinner in the world who'd like to have moments in heaven as they'd be kneeling on the pews to pray, with their eyes, hearts, and souls filled with awe, gratitude, and rejoicing. How my husband would look at the church with much resplendent faith. I clutch the Holy Rosary though I cannot pray from too much pain and unforgivable regret! How often did I mock my husband's faith when I was seethed with ire, with the egotistic derring-do for vengeance over human atrocity! If only…if only…

OASIS. This is blissful stop over for every tired and hungry traveller. They have the best of Ilocano dishes! From *siningang na malaga*, to *bopis* or *igado* to *dinardaraan, dinakdakan*, to *kalderetang kambing* and *sinanglaw*, they serve it, including again, the hot bowls of heaven. Enzo would just relish all the flavours and be thankful to the *Manongs* and *Manangs* for their fine cooking, their exotic condiments, and magical flavorings. "Mama, *ang sarap kumain dito sa Oasis!*" My husband would cheerfully tell me, his taste buds content, his heart beating nice and well while my heart keeps the memories with little JP running to check on our pets who are sleeping soundly in their own contentment, with the fresh air blowing cool and invigorating. But now the L300 just speeds fast through the once favorite Ilocano restaurant of my husband. I wipe my tears, my soul groans in the pits of incomparable dolor, with my lonely innocent little son sleeping on my lap of unimaginable regret and remorse! I should have been a much better wife, cooking more often my husband's favorite vivers and victuals while learning to just do efficient minimal marking of my students' essays! How we could've made a lot more of crazy fantastic love out from that economics of grammar checking! For most times, we'd just foreplay with translations for the hours were scarce for amazing conjugal bliss as the endless piles of papers just stole so much from our supposed moments of conjugal sublimation!

SAN JUAN, LA UNION. The surfing paradise of tourists and locals. How we used to say in sheer astonishment, *"Ang daming turista! Bakit puro barbecue eh Good Friday?"* One time we managed to go home to Ilocos for the Holy Week but it was already Good Friday. It was around dinner time when we were driving along the famous tourist destination. We were just so relieved to see a lot of people and bright lights after the long stretches of darkness and no humanity in sight. But we had a question in our hearts. However, our faith in God told us not to judge neither be judgmental, and to be more understanding, open-minded, of course, not to dwell on the sin neither the sinner but to love even when in doubt for the grace of charitable faith comes like the sea breeze, blowing and flowing freely even in the lairs and the crevices of danger, of the tents of crime, of the palaces of the contemptible. God's love, as our hearts have known in the many years of our love story as sweethearts and then as husband and wife, does not exclude anyone. His love for all His creations is all embracing and forgiving; it's really all up to us if we'd respond to that love, value it, and die with it. Enzo, my husband died with God's love and his love and devotion for Our Mother of Perpetual Help as he'd pray the Holy Rosary each morning in the hospital and he never would let go of his Novena Prayer Book, even when they took him to that fateful TURP surgery. He clutched it so tight that the OR and Recovery Room nurses kept it and gave it then to me. Even when life was good and perfect, my husband would never fail to pray his devotion to Our Blessed Mother, the Holy Rosary, and they were always in his pocket. My tears remember the man who loved me for what I was at twenty-nine years old until I've gotten some of those gray hair, including all my faults and my shortcomings. He just simply loved me. I cry again as the L300 continues to handle the road in the speed of uncompromising irreversible reality.

TAGUDIN, ILOCOS SUR. At this point, I am already suicidal. My body wants to throw itself over the long white bridge to end its torture, its fatigue, all of its memories. "Mama, *nasa* Ilocos Sur *na tayo! Salamat po, Panginoon*, Our Mother of Perpetual Help!" My husband always says these words of joyful gratitude once we'd enter the mouth of the Ilocos Sur Bridge. The L300 is speeding even more as if it's flying, too excited to reach home! My heart goes berserk, my soul writhes in much greater gnawing pain that my hands tremble as I see in my memory the faces of those medical malpractitioners! My tears just won't stop anymore until they begin to dry up, and my torture is like the man with the thirty pieces of silver! I now howl like the fox of the coldest regions on Earth! The bald driver steals worried glances on the widow whose child rouses from the sudden loud so loud wailings of his sleepless grieving, mourning, remorseful mother. As the sun makes its highest climb, the widow sees all the episodes of her almost twenty-five years of life then with the man who is now in the white casket, in that L300 that's flying in the scorching heat, wanting to beat the seconds of time…

He knew by heart every single town of my home province. He never mistook one for the other; each one was special! "Emy, *ang ganda ng sinilangan mong probinsiya!* Ilocos Sur is one of a kind!" Enzo, my boyfriend just can't hide his admiration for my homeprovince as we're on the red and white Times Transit bus. This is December 1992. It's our fourth month as lovers. *"Anong bayan ito? Kalamay ba iyong mga iyon?"* Enzo is more than ecstatic to taste the native delicacies of Candon, Ilocos Sur. This town would then become a frequent, regular stop over for our family of three with our zoo, our travelling menagerie in the many years of our seasons in marvellous grace. Our little son JP would then try to pronounce the town's name as he was learning the vowels and the consonants but would fail many times to pronounce CANDON, and say it with a letter T at the middle and at the end of the word that his father would then cover his mouth[as in Filipino, that orthography and spelling redound to a vulgar!], and then rehearse with him the name of the town over and over again. I make a tearful little laugh, and JP asks me why as I remember those fun times in our family life. The bald driver again makes furtive glances on the widow, obviously bothered and perplexed.

SAN ESTEBAN AND SANTA MARIA. "Mama and JP, be careful! Watch your steps!" My husband is as equally excited for little Joseph Mary Peter Paul Lamb as he's about to make his first adventure in the sea. I remove his shoes, and carry my three year old to the waiting blue and green water. I dip him fast, I dip him much lower, I dip him more and more lest I forget to dip those heels like the mythological Achilles and his mother! My son laughs in joy and upon sight of the small and colourful school of fish swimming around him. Enzo approaches us laughing with our Labrador, Linda Cassiopeia which by now, also wants to plunge in the beautiful sea. I sigh in the memory of such wonderful moment as my eyes get a glimpse of that circle of rocks and water where the happy family of that yesterday had their frolic and carefree. My tears begin to swell in my eyes again, the sore blight and affliction of my soul mount the horrible bellows of self-blame and guilt for reckless impudent temper! But how my husband loved me even when I was totally worthless!

NARVACAN. "Oh God, please help me! Most Immaculate Heart of

Mary pray for me and my son! Most Sacred Heart of Jesus, have mercy upon us!" My heart is beating too fast and too powerful I can die now! This town would see my husband beginning to fret for the keys of our home while I'd handle the fork, the intersection, one to uphill formidable Abra, while the other to the town of the most fresh of catch[like the rare fish, *ipon*!], the town of farmers, fishermen, carpenters, and of dreamers. THE CLOCK TICKS NOT FOR THE LIVING BUT FOR THE LIVING DEAD, TO QUICKLY TURN THE HANDS OF TIME FOR THE THOUSANDS OF HOURS SPENT WITH LOVE'S FAITHFUL KISSES! SO LONG AND ADIEUS BUT NONE BRINGS BACK THE SMILE OF ROSES! I

SANTA, ILOCOS SUR. We are now in my hometown, where I was born. The two stone kissing fish by the curve signals the entry to the smallest town of the province but for many decades, would produce the most number of professionals. This is the boundary between two Ilocos Sur towns kissed incessantly by the China Sea, of their friendly and dangerous[shallow then deep, deep then shallow] shorelines. "The more than three-decade life size statue of the Blessed Mother on top of a huge rock, with her open, embracing hands to the vastness of the blue sea and the skies, glistens in the radiant sun though it seems to mourn as the L300 passes and makes its serpent-like motion in time. "JP, where's the flashlight?" My husband would then cheerfully panic to look for the keys of our conjugal family home. His joy is all over his face, his body, his language. He'd clap his hands like a child the moment he sees the town's landmark, and his eyes, the glow of a contented husband, a happy man married to an Ilocana, raised at the foot of a mystical mountain, *SLEEPING BEAUTY*. The L300 is unstoppable and unmindful of the dangers of the sharp curves and zig zags. My whole being quivers. I begin to float. My body tears and cuts in pieces. The L300 is now traversing the much higher ground, the road along the Santa Public Cemetery. My mother, my grandmother, and my sister shed their tears for my travelling dead husband; and for now, my fatherless son, and for me, a remorseful widow! How often did I abuse and exploit the GOODNESS of the man who loved me when I never deserved to be loved by such a man? How many times did I ruin supposedly more blissful times of our marriage, of our family life if I learned to manage better my ill temper, my jealousy, my pride, my PMS[pre-menstrual, post-menstrual, my menopause[!] and spoiled brat-*wifey* ways, even my inefficient budgeting?! I am now the wretched fate of my own sins! The crawling *kadena de amor* grieves with my soul as the famous/infamous winds, *"Umatiberret ti angin diay Santa!"*, howl with the terrors and horrors of my unabated, escalatingly devastating, overpowering woe; I AM THE LIVING DEAD. INDEED, INDEED, I AM, I AM!

We now overtake the L300 to lead the way to the lonely convoy. I cannot even swallow my pain, and my mouth is just too dry. "Mama, the pharmacist was teasing me with my crisp twenty-peso bills! *Sabi niya, sapin na ba iyon ng* wallet ko! Hahaha!" My husband has been good friends through the years with all the *Manongs* and the *Manangs,* including the Pharmacy Board Topnotcher teasing woman of *Ninoy's* Family Drug. That's how beautiful and humble was the heart of the man I married twice! Heaven feels the unforgivable pain of the once overly spoiled wife who so abused the overwhelming love and patience of her late husband!

THE STRAIGHT ROAD TO RIZAL, SANTA. Silver Angel speeds through it. The green house of our father that sits on a more than three thousand square meter-lot at the foot of the legendary majestic mountain is closed and empty. We now climb the road, and oh, we pass by the Rizal Chapel! I suddenly shout to the bald man to make a turn. I turn my head to the trailing L300. It now makes a slow careful turn and waits right in front of the *Barangay's* Chapel in beige, chocolate brown, and dark green where *KRISTO REY,* Christ The King sits on the Holy Altar with the Blessed Mother. My heart is beating like war drums, the bugle calls to eternal sorrow and pain. The two vehicles take the short narrow road to the open fields until A HOUSE of faded lavender roof, purple gate, and more than a dozen maroon windows. My husband is finally HOME. The Indian Mangoes are quiet though watchful and prayerful in the high noon of Good Friday.

They are all standing in a row by the old rose and gray terrace like silhouettes of the sorrowful men and women of Jesus, the Nazarene thousands of years ago. My father is teary-eyed, my brothers Elrey and Errol Anthony are teary-eyed too, all the men and young men of our family are with tearful eyes. My sisters are crying, weeping, sobbing, including all the little ones while the babies coo as if they knew the elegy of pain. The

L300 opens its back door. The men of St. Peter's and of our family carry the white casket out of the vehicle very carefully, and move to the terrace of memories, until our *sala*, now with the funeral home's bright lights, white curtains and flowing white cloth with a huge Holy Cross of Jesus at the middle of all these. My Enzo is home, my Enzo is home. Today is the fourteenth of April 2017. Good Friday. *Biyernes Santo*…my dead husband is home…**I shall but forfeit the memory for the cauldron of my sanity cans't bear the BLEEDING OF ROSES…the horrors of perfect love strike as lightning to the swaying boughs of April…no fowls in the air dare measure the heights of terror, no minstrel attempts to trudge about in the caves of despair…just the widow's tears…just the widow's tears…**

THE BLACK SERPENT And "The Taming Of The Shrew"

The eyes look at me then it's gone.

"Mama, Mama, *may ahas, may ahas!!!*" JP shouts running towards me. It's summer 2018. We just got back from the city. My summer classes just ended, with my graduate students sending their final papers to Ilocos via LBC. I run fast to check on my son, then scamper for a long bamboo stick. The snake on the grass is the longest sleek black I've ever seen! We grew up almost playing with baby snakes, screaming upon sight of their mothers in yellow and green; in sheer astonishment for large chicken-eaters, the *banas* with fat bellies which the old folks would then turn and cook into exotic dishes or simply *kilawin* while they drank their *basi* or bottles of *sioktong* under the moonlight. But this one is black, the first one ever! Then, in a second, it moves so gracefully fast. "Mama, quick! *Paluin mo na sa ulo!*" JP cries out loud from our dirty kitchen. I make the first strike, and I hit the sleek body. He moves fast and then stops before our *Bahay Kubo*. Then he turns his head on me, so poised, the INEXPLICABLE AWE! My God, he's perfect, perfectly beautiful! His long slender body is a shimmering black in the ray of the afternoon sun. "Mama, *patayin mo na! Anong ginagawa mo, Mama?*" My eleven year-old son is now impatient with his mother! I hesitate but I then raise my bamboo stick to make the kill. My heart tells me to let him be. The sleek black moves in the ode of life. I then sat by the tomb of my beloved by the Grotto of Our Mother Mary, by the Dorantha,[for my Lawrence of Arabia!], and by the rustling Indian Mangoes at midnight, while the full moon and a myriad of stars listened to my confessions, my remorse, my regret, my woes and my pains as well as my songs, my hymns, my petitions, and my prayers of thanksgiving. By the first day of June, 2018, I have made my first Facebook posting, my fight for justice for my husband killed from medical malpractice. I am now by this time, FB literate. The drizzle of the other night, June 1, 2018 brought the miracle of GREAT TRUE LOVE. As the black and maroon tomb glistened in the falling rain, my fingers were guided by the handsome ghost of my beloved while I sat overnight at the terrace of our dreams. By October 2018, I've discovered my first book doing well in the world market. And around this date, I would then be reunited to my first UP Diliman professor after thirty-five years. By February 2019,.

However, my CROWNING OF THORNS would continue as I struggle both with my intense sorrow and the burden of raising my child and sending him to a good school in the face of great financial crisis, as all of our family's savings have depleted and gone with the irony of fate, and to add insult to injury, with my well-deserved job of thirteen years deprived from me by unfeeling humanity, cruel episodes of widow and orphan thrown out of their apartment with their old but very precious belongings for the beautiful memories, by self-centered, heartless oligarchy, their family van scratched, vandalized, tires deflated by egotistic men just because mother and child got the better legal parking on the city street, their old but very special red Hyundai being the object of ire, intimidation, and hostility by *machos en honchos* [but thank you to the kind, compassionate, and very helpful handy man, Toto and the UP Gym security guards for taking care of our old car right there in the campus for almost a year without asking anything in return! These men are truly shining examples that today, there are still many good eggs in the basket!]. While I fight the daily temptations of suicide from overwhelming pain, regret, remorse, and despair of losing the only man I've ever loved, THE MAN WHO WILLINGLY GENEROUSLY AND TRULY LOVED ME in good times or in bad times, with the PMS, the menopause, or the bad hair, lingering in bed or a couch potato, oh, even with the little and ugly demons sticking out of my wits and piquant tongue, or the incontrollable gas, my love for my child and his love for me, his mother, our pets, their sweet compassionate purring and barking, the promises of every new day, the lovely photos, notes, cards, gifts, books, and loving memories of my husband, the thoughtful sincere prayers, gestures, and kindness of family and friends, even of total strangers, the gentle face and embracing arms of Mother Mary, the WORDS OF JESUS, THE MAN ON THE CROSS, just make me strong enough to bear all the bleeding…as the long hours, the painful days, the months of misery, the years of MISSING THE BELOVED begin to count with the silent tears…and the unwritten memoirs in the Terrace of Old Rose Memories…what greater sorrow, what greater sorrow not to forget the face of a dead beloved inside the casket… but greatest is the sorrow to unforget the last kiss…I know a thousand and more years shall tame my pain…in that PERFECT MOMENT…

## TO LOVE WITH THE BIRDS

Today is 28 May 2019. I am now at the last chapter of my fourth book. The tomb of my husband is just a few steps away. I am writing in our very quiet *azotea*. A few stems of *Sampaguita* lie in magically incantational, incantatory bliss on my *Kamagong*[Mahogany] writing table, my husband's old study and dining table in UP while we were not yet married by the Judge and the Jesuit. My sister, Estela Marie who lives alone by herself in our very old almost falling family house brings me the immaculate blossoms of May, every day like I were to parade in the *Flores de Mayo* or *Santacruzan*. She puts them on my table while I'm still sleeping in the blistering high noon as I do not sleep anymore at night…

Oh, here the downpour comes! The first of May. I see myself somewhere as my much younger spinster sister waters the veranda plants! Perhaps, Nick Joaquin's "May Day Eve" is on her, or she's as odd and eccentric as her lowly author of an older sibling. But Estela Marie is always herself, very gracious, with her cactus, with her bonsai, with her pot holders, with her *Sampaguitas*. She is beautiful in her simple existence. And I love her so. My sister Ely, too who cooks all the finest dishes, noodles, *putos*, and the shrubs of paradise! Her eyes always sparkle with some inebriated but grateful tear. She now takes care of her *apos*[grandchildren]while she continues to live her life of devotion to her husband, Guiller, a handy man, Jack of all trades, worked day and night to build that bridge connecting Santa to Bantay, an unsung hero[!], and once worked as an overseas Filipino worker[OFW] in KSA, plus of course, their four children, three with their respective families, making my sister's hands always full but her pride of her big family gives her all the contentment of being a woman. Oh, how I envy her for the beautiful and happy noise of her home! Her life makes me think more often now every dusk and daybreak if it was all worth it spending so much time in the city, on my books, on my Ph.D. when I could have gotten married much earlier, to build happily that sweet nidus, that nest of true great love, to get more those bundles of joy, all those babies, have lots of fun time with my husband while feeding the pets, planting *utong ken kabatiti* in our backyard, gossiping with the locals on a pleasant day, and perhaps writing dozens of biographies, of memoirs under the moonlight while reading more of the timeless romance on vines, of course, for as long as I can still afford climbing my trees of comfort and delight like the tireless conduits of pismires, carrying all those morsels, feasting on the piroshki, or those cute playful rabbits enjoying the carrot and the chervil in their little corners as the rains come! My sighs never end as sunsets and mornings give me head-on collisions with life and its givens. Being a widow is such an occasion for the poetry of discernment, the penchant for the pungent and the poignant, aside of course, from the infinite punishing eternity of the paradoxical conflict and riddle of UNFORGETTING. Ah, my younger sisters and their lives add to the *espiglere*, the *verité*, the pixilation and vitality of my lowly little pen and likewise the nurse who worked in Tripoli. Our eldest is always in her cocoon [though happier and more at peace in her retirement age!] which used to be covered by the thick foliage of our old *Salamagi* [Tamarind tree]that carried with it a very naughty tale of bantering and smart aleck of youthful sisters. *Manang* Baby Lou and *Manang* Erleen tried to outsmart each other in climbing the tree, resulting to our much older sister, Baby Lou accidentally hurt by the stunned *pina* [pineapple]underneath the *Sampaloc* [Tamarind tree]. Oh, I was barely eight but I remember too vividly how our *Mamang* Lourdes cursed youthful silliness and juvenile delinquency in sporadic Castilian lexis as she gave first aid to our eldest sibling! The wild rare blue orchid, my partner in many youthful adventures and crimes was then made to lie flat on her face on our bright red sofa, and received her corporal punishment of the brown leather belt with the huge golden buckle, just like how I received mine when we escaped to swim in the beautiful but dangerous Banaoang/ Abra River, and I lost my little *katya* [undies] to the current! Our father, a young government executive at the time would not tolerate any *kalokohan* [mischief]! *Manang* Baby Lou is now also a widow after our *Batangueno,* brother-in-law, *Kuya* Lino Guce fell in a deep hole from his fatal heart attack! He had a nice native Batangas accent and he never learned to speak Ilocano[unlike *Ate* Fe, his M.D. younger sister married to Mayor Hernaiz of Sta. Lucia] in more than five decades of living in Ilocandia, the perfect example of Howard Giles' linguistic divergence! He and our eldest sister met and fell in love in Tripoli, Libya while our *Ate* worked there as a nurse. The youngest of my sisters, Ethel Consuelo, married to Emilson, an airplane mechanic, posts recently of her conviction of the story of true love, real as it is, never ends...

I'm fifty-five and I don't fart that much anymore. But, I've become a coffee-addict. Without my three-in-one, I panic and I weep. Maybe another little biography or fiction? My pen gives me all that I need... somehow...Except a man. But I don't need one. I've had the best...

How he loved me and how I loved him. I still do. FOREVER...

I went to the Pink Sisters' Convent in the New Manila area in 1992. While Enzo taught as SEASSI Fulbright Lecturer at the University of Washington, Seattle, U.S.A. I wrote on a note my petition and prayer for my GREAT TRUE LOVE. I asked the Lord, "Please protect him from any harm. If he is for me then please give him back to me!"

Around 1995, I asked again the Pink Sisters, this time in their Baguio City Convent[where they make the most divine strawberry and _ube_ jams!] to include in their novenas my petition, "Jesus, if he's for me then help us get married!" I was with the Benedictine monks, my San Beda College family at that time. Oh, the monks just gave me some of the best times of my life as when one amazing afternoon, I was literally talking on the phone with my boyfriend while I was standing on crocodile farm in Palawan!

From 1992, almost every year, my then boyfriend and myself would go to so many chapels and churches, including shrines, seminaries, and of course, convents to pray together, and petition for our love for each other, God's blessings of good health, prosperity, and our much awaited matrimony! Enzo would take me to a shrine in Antipolo after our visit of the miraculous and famous, Our Lady Of Antipolo that sits up there almost at the apex of the church, climbing a very high staircase that I would then have nightmares of falling from heaven [Jesus! Maybe, I was just too guilty for my little and big sins! I had my m.u.'s or mutual understandings, around two or three, but they were too innocent [though one was *espial* and *pixie*!], and simply, all puppy love or harmless, *espiegle* adventure in the spring time of life! Oh, I've always been odd, I think and hence, my extraordinary tastes! But of course I am more than grateful for these boys were perfect gentlemen and were never inclined to date rapes, what with my cute little dagger ready for the defense of Bataan!

The shrine had huge statues of the sorrowful mysteries. Enzo and I would then take photos of each other kneeling beside Jesus at the Garden of Gethsemane[not really knowing what and how that kneeling felt and meant!], until the Lord's crucifixion at the top of a small hill. This visit was our first in 1992 which would then be followed by a few more, bringing then with us *Manang* Erleen, her kids, and some more of our little nephews and nieces. My sister was overwhelmed by the very peaceful yet too spiritually uplifting sacred place that she'd flash her happiest smiles and poses before the camera especially beside the nailed Jesus! However, in 1999, I would then dream of her and our *Auntie* Lita being inside beautiful caskets! My sister passed away on October 5, 2005, while our aunt would pass on a year or two later. I never told my sister of my dream for she had always known something was queer of her little favorite sister, and I just didn't want to spoil her fun in the sun!

"Oh, he's driving way too fast! Oh my God! He gets out of the windshield!" I don't know but I told my stepmother, Consuelo or *Tita* Chelie of my dream. Her brother, a lawyer, would then have a fatal car accident on that same place where I saw him die in my dream. He fell out of the windshield from the impact of the accident. Many knew of this odd tragic dream as our stepmother related it to her family.

"Believe me, she's got her bouncing baby!" I just exclaimed to my unbelieving *Manang* Erleen that her sister-in-law based in L.A. California has delivered her first child. Then her other sister-in-law comes in a split second to bring the good news of the cute and robust Indian baby! On the other hand, I'd then see earth with cracks and plants in crevices on a huge foot, like of a giant, in my bedroom, as I switch on the lights coming from

Sunday evening mass. Days later, the big earthquake of 1990 would then take place, with me on top of some rocks surrounded by plants, holding the little hands of crying Maryknoll Grade Schoolers, about a dozen of them whom I led to that open space but in a garden!

I see her so pretty seated in a corner, bantering with her male classmate. Oh, why do I see her now dying in a hospital! She was my UST Tourism freshman student, Maricel. She died two months later on her hospital bed from chronic asthma! I wipe my tears as I look at her beautiful face in her coffin. Three years earlier, Ina, my Maryknoller student says good-bye to me as she kisses me on my cheek, and I then get to see her so beautiful but lying dead on some street. That was a Friday. By Monday, I'd then learn that my dear sweet Ina died on a car accident along SM North, her pretty face destroyed as their car skidded some thirty meters on the road.

"Oh God!" My English 12 class shouts in shock. The huge entire glass window crashes hard on the ground. The Ateneo de Manila security and personnel come running. It was almost October 2005. My sister Erleen was now dying from brain cancer. I was feeling too bad at the time of my class though of course, I loved my *Atenistas* who made my five years of teaching in ADMU greatly fulfilling. What overflowing brilliance and talents that should see the nation up on its feet to global prominence, leadership, and progress! The following meeting, it was the wall fan that suddenly fell in that same class. My sister would then die on October 5, a week after the incident, and I would then resign from the university. In 2009, as I cooked and prepared the Noche Buena[around 10 o'clock in the evening, with the usual strong winds of Santa!] for our big family in Ilocos, my eyes would get to see outside the open windows a very beautiful woman standing there, wearing a pink dress, all made up for the family gathering and reunion! She's smiling but doesn't look me in the eye. She did the same on her 40th day in 2005! My husband and I were bringing home to UP my friend, Cherry who was seated alone at the back of our car but as I was managing the humps and looked at the rear mirror, I saw her beside my friend, this time she was wearing her white hospital gown, she looked very sad, but she didn't look at me. I then pulled over and cried to the obvious fright of my friend, and making my husband speechless. There are more but let me just keep them in my heart…besides, I feel I've shocked you more than maybe you'd imagined before flipping the pages of my autobiography…however, may I recount of one very magical though again bizarre experience and little ones around it…

"Is that you, Enzo? I ask in the dimly lighted room of our new family house that's almost at the foot of the mysterious *Sleeping* Beauty Mountain. But my boyfriend is snoring beside me! I just saw a tall man with curly hair and a cap, *tabako* [*long* tobacco] in his mouth, sneering at me from outside our curtained green room. But the windows were open wide as Enzo and I wanted the mountain breeze to come in as we slept. At around two a.m., the air was then blowing hard as well as the electric fan, making the pastel floral curtains to move like they were waving kites. I froze as I saw the stranger, that I closed my eyes in fright while I tried to rouse my boyfriend who was obviously in deep sleep! Whenever I'd see the supernatural even in younger days, I'd just simply close my eyes and murmur the Lord's Prayer though I just couldn't do the same one late stormy night of October 31, 2003 while I was driving with Enzo in our Hyundai sedan to Ilocos Sur, with so many long-haired women in white standing by the roadside! We almost had a head-on collision with a big bus as I was too frightened, I drove to the other lane! Going back to the huge creature which seemingly had a crush on me, heavens[!], maybe he saw me from where he was hiding while I was in dreamland, my childhood habit! Days before this odd scary thing happened I fell asleep and long, one lazy afternoon on the *papag* [wooden bed] under the Carabao Mango trees that surrounded [and still they do!] our father's all green house. At this time, everyone was real busy preparing for the house blessing, with the entire *barangay* or village to attend it; *Papang, Tita* Chelie, Errol Anthony, and Ethel Consuelo just moved in to their new abode. As usual, I was again daydreaming of my boyfriend who was still in Manila for he still had his summer classes in UP Diliman. Then I just dozed off in the magical phantom of a legendary afternoon. When I woke up, it was almost supper, the moon was large and low. The mountain breeze felt like the majestic mountain's soft and gentle breathing, and in the moonlight, *Sleeping Beauty* smiled at me, with the shadows of the Mango trees dancing like happy *tikbalangs* and *kapres* [Philippine supernatural creatures]! I then made the sign of the cross and prayed the Angelus. I will never forget that mystic rhapsody of a lifetime…hidden worlds…special ones…strange creatures…queer, very queer but they've come real…even in succeeding years, I'd feel something eerie, weird, efferent once the world was asleep until late last year, 2018, while I'd be writing short memoirs for my beloved as if the huge creature was just outside the maroon windows, watching the widow struggle with her pains...or when it's full moon, and she sits wiping her tears until daybreak by the tomb of her Enzo, the "stranger" seems to be hiding in the dark, either on those huge farm trees nearby or behind the swaying bamboo trees across my writing spot. In our town SANTA, many strange [oh!] things seem to happen during and several days after the full moon as this quiet small town, nestled at the foot of the great legendary mountain, is the birthplace of dreamers...or, just maybe...I am the Full Moon's Daughter[!], that I had seen my husband already walking as a ghost one night I was cleaning the cages though he was still very much alive! I told him but a bit of the story in 2016 as I was just too scared it might happen... but the inevitable cruelty of fate came...time and destiny are always the immortal hands of both bliss and suffering. They never come and go without leaving their marks and scars.

Indeed, I've been there. We were there. My husband Enzo, our child JP, myself, our little zoo, our menagerie. We lived "close" to the Holy Manger. But, we didn't know. We just felt the joy, the bliss, even the dangers. Enzo had his own world before we met, I had mine too. Until our worlds came together, and our child was born in that manger nearby His Holiness. Linda Cassiopeia came with her BRIGHTEST LIGHT. Then Kitty to lead us all to that road, to THE TRAIL, that HEAVEN on Earth. She was a noble cat who walked in our home with the GREATEST TALE to bring us, to help us make it come to life, while we were busy cleaning each cage, morning and evening, calm or rage, ordinary or special occasions, in sin or in our saint, JERUSALEM WAS REAL...

It's been two years since Enzo passed away. I still cry, I still weep, and I still sin. Yes, that sunset was treacherous! The first ever sunset we watched with our feet kissed by the little waves of the vast China Sea, the sea of my childhood, of my youth, of my dreams. The three of us sat on a rock as we waited for the sun to disappear in the hands of time. Enzo held my hand so lovingly, and I felt the glory of eternity while little JP played with the cold blue green. That afternoon, that dusk filled my heart with so much joy and gratitude. Those moments, I thought and felt, were forever...From a distance, a priest, and a nun...from far away Bangladesh, with gifts of the best mantles and table cloths! They were with us in those times, those golden moments of our lives. St. Catherine Church would just be waiting nearby the sea, in a simple square of prayerful townsfolk, many of whom are fishermen, farmers, carpenters, *bolo makers* [blacksmith], blanket-weavers, and teachers. Jesus was then preparing the way...the road much closer to Bethlehem...I was unaware...Enzo was unaware...our child was being blessed for the journey to the real JERUSALEM...

Now, as I look back of that life I had shared with such a good man for almost twenty-five years, I am filled with the Grace of Love; the marriage that bound us for thirteen years fills me with the Grace of Thanksgiving; the home that all three of us made and with our pets fills me with the Grace of Everlasting Glory; my tears, my remorse, my woes, my memoirs, my books, they fill me with the Grace of Penitence...

The Roads to the Real Jerusalem are indeed but many. They may be a child's, a father's, a mother's, a brother's, a sister's, a grandparent's, a relative's, a friend's, a stranger's, a family's; they may be the religious life, the married life, the single-blessedness, the single-parent's, the widowhood. They can be so ordinary, so old, so forgotten, or so special, so new, so familiar. They can come with the good winds and the storms; they can come with the blissful joys and the tears or even with the mystic phenomenons. The Roads to Jerusalem may have all those golden flowers, those rare shrubs and special reeds, those wonderful herbs, those lovely plants, and those glorious trees...or those sharp thorns and poisonous serpents and terrifying wolves. Yes, now I know the roads are never just one. There are many but all converge at some special point, on THE TRAIL of Joseph, Mary, and the CHILD in her womb, with the lowly but loyal donkey, and the guiding light of the great star. The Gift of Jerusalem is for everyone...

"Mili, *sabali ka nga talaga, kakatwa*[odd]!" How many times I'd hear of this remark from my *Manang* Erleen while we were growing up. Our *Lilang* Andang would say, "*nasyaat ta ar-aramidem apok! maragsakan ni Apo Hesus!*"[God is pleased with you, grandchild!]. *Mamang* Lourdes tells me then," *nasirib ti anak ko!*[My child has good head on her shoulders!]. My father would say, "*Nasyaat ngarud nakkong!*[Good job, my daughter!]. My husband then writes me, "You are very special, and I love you!" The rest of humanity would have other more words to say.

The tragic death of my husband would throw me many times in hell.

I'd curse endlessly with my heart full of rage, and with all the violence in my head. I'd imagine how I would slay with my claws, attack with my dagger, smite with my sword! I'd entertain the devil, Lucifer in my dreams, in my nightmares. I'd wallow in the rivers of blood, my soul refusing heaven! The blows came to me real and merciless. I was on the ground that cared nothing even of my single tear. The black serpent came and I was dazed, bewitched, beguiled, bedazzled; I was once more beaten by the blows of treachery, of cruel deception, of the horrors of my woes. I've been wandering too far away from JERUSALEM...

UNTIL one day.

He was walking in the strides of a man of the fields. He had his *bolo* dangling in his torn working short pants, the dutiful hands feeling the farm, the crops, the growing grass as the air blew its ode to the hardworking fellow, named KULAS. I was again at the top of my voice, screaming my wrath and woes to the universe. I've just buried my husband in that year, 2017, on the 26th of April, in the familiar ground, that exact spot he would loved then every night to stand long, gazing at the moon, the sky, and the stars, while holding the chain of our dog, Linda Cassiopeia in one hand. And how he loved the desert beauty, Dorantha and her purple flowers, a real Lawrence of Arabia! The Indian Mangoes, how he'd happily stand underneath their gracious boughs, touching, holding those marvels of the soil and all of nature's splendor, such poetry of joyful contentment and grateful prayerful smiles on his lips! Yes, I buried my beloved Enzo where his heart had always whispered its secrets, wishes, and prayers... very much like Robert Louis Stevenson's "Here he lies where he longed to be"... with his Novena to Our Mother of Perpetual Help, bearing that precious wooden cross. I quickly put his prayer leaflet on his left hand and ran away as fast as I could before they sealed his tomb, my heart bleeding oceans of deepest sorrow, with all the sharpest daggers GREAT TRUE LOVE could ever take and bear! So, that hot afternoon, when the wind just couldn't seem to ignore the widow's cries for justice for her fallen beloved, heaven heard her wailings, her curses, her distress, and her pleas for help! The wind took her cause to divine ears! And while nobody seemed to mind her except for lips that whispered ill, doors that opened and shut, school children who stared at her as if she was some odd and dangerous museum, the wind blew, whirled, and took the widow's woes to Mt. Calvary! "In my distress

I cried unto the Lord and he heard me."[Psalm 120:1] At that moment, the black and maroon granite was a lot more quiet but it was listening with the dead husband's tears falling on that ground where his wife used to play and dream as a little child, while the Yellow Bells, the Dorantha, and the Indian Mangoes just let themselves prance in the air, in the rhythm of the widow's cries, fury, and elegy. And when the widow continued to lash out to the universe for its frustrating *WALANG PAKIALAM* [indifference] attitude to medical malpractice, its apathy, its lethargy for the silent piteous victims lying in vain in their tombs for elusive justice, with their families left to battle on their own the very powerful nexuses or forces, her lungs almost bursting in too much anger and distress, then, the VOICE OF THE OPEN FIELDS SPOKE, and gave the widow the Wisdom of Kulas: *"Manang, bay-amon. Kasta la ti biag. Adda nasyaat, adu ti madi. Haan mo nga padagsenen ta barukong mo!"*[Ma'am, just let things be. Life has good and bad. Don't burden yourself too much!].

Oh Jesus Christ, the farmer brought me back on my Road to Jerusalem! I was just too struck by the eloquence, the radiance of his wisdom, the good man of the soil, of the most humble of clothes, of the most ordinary of men! His truth hit me hard and deep for it was downright genuine, his heart sounded so pure! My heart was overwhelmed with remorse! "I have gone astray like a lost sheep..." [Tau 176]. Yes, what have I done with the Grace of Life for almost two years? What have I been doing with the precious moments of sunrise and the poetry of seven hundred and thirty of sunsets? Indeed, my husband is gone! He is back with the Father, his Creator and his God. I have been disturbing his eternal sleep; I've not been really praying for his peaceful repose as too much anger and the desire for vengeance have gripped my heart and soul in that stretch of time! I've just been cursing the world and sinning and sinning more, hurting my son, my family, everyone with my pain, my depression, bitterness, cowardice, and wrath! I have allowed Lucifer to take me to hell, again and again, for every second I'd play over and over in my head how I'd avenge my beloved in every full moon of my agony! "I am for peace:but when I speak, they are for war."[Psalm 120:7]." But this lowly man, this very simple ordinary man just made me realize I've become a dreadful beast on my way to JERUSALEM! I've become my own evil! I've lost track of my direction! "If I forget thee, O Jerusalem, let my right hand forget her cunning. If I do not remember thee, let my tongue cleave to the roof of my mouth; if I prefer not Jerusalem above my chief joy."[Psalm 137:5-6] I've forgotten to oil my lamp! Kulas taught me in such Grace of Random Moment to live again with his smile that spoke of his faith in life, and that life resonates truth; the good and the bad as well as the choice, and the humility to Carry One's Cross to Mt. Calvary. Yes, the MIRACLE OF SALVATION begins in Jerusalem as ETERNITY has so declared! One should strive to purify oneself as The Child In The Manger was born to Mary and Joseph to SAVE the world but has to DIE IN THE CROSS. From that afternoon with THE FARMER, I started to accept death, though still with so much anguish yet with greater REVERENCE for the death of my beloved, the Gift of Mortality...the Will of God as I was gradually led since that moment in time to recognize of my own life's transitoriness, of everyone's, no matter who we are, regardless of what we do and what we are, that life on earth must end to begin A LIFE OF ETERNAL HAPPINESS WITH JESUS where burdens, tears, and pains are no more but hymns of exaltation to the Most High! "I will praise thee with my whole heart:before the gods will I sing praise unto thee."[Psalm 138:1] But of course, acceptance is a process, a Work of Grace! Not ever to forget that with the Grace of Forgiveness and Reconciliation is a genuinely totally CONTRITE HEART that CONFESSES THE CRIME OF SIN, before God and in the courts or congregations of men! "Those who love the Lord hate evil." [Psalm 97]. Charity has to be preceded by JUSTICE, for humanity has to carry its own burden before the promise of the RESURRECTION OF JESUS! While each one of us is welcome upon the assembly, to behold the great throne of HEAVEN, we need to SUFFER the brunt of our sins for us to earn entry to the KINGDOM OF GOD, that cool spot to ETERNAL HAPPINESS. "The fear of the Lord is the beginning of wisdom:a good understanding have all they that do his commandments:his praise endureth forever." [Psalm 111]. JERUSALEM teaches and reminds us that to share in the GLORY OF GOD is to face and handle the dangers, the fears, and the doubts. To run away is to stay far from the Divine Mercy of the Father! The PASCHAL MYSTERY is most perfect and beautiful upon the CONVERSION OF SINNERS, for didn't Jesus become incarnate to save the sick among men, the sinners? From His birth, the NATIVITY, to His PASSION, the Father's promise of salvation is fulfilled. But we need to humble ourselves, CONFESS AND REPENT FOR OUR SINS, and open our hearts to the GRACE OF SALVATION FROM CHRIST'S DEATH AND RESURRECTION. "I will behave myself wisely in a perfect way. O when wilt thou come unto me? I will walk within my house with a perfect heart."[Psalm 101:2]. It is not easy, it may not come easy but our own salvation depends on us, on how we respond to God's divine mercy and love, with our free will, our inner voice, our conscience. "I will say of the Lord, He is my refuge and my fortress:my God in him will I trust."[Psalm 91:2] While we have the second, the moment, the now, we must take courage to pay for our sins by carrying our own crosses to the Mountain of Salvation. As what had been written in the sacred scriptures, God is experienced in the mountain like Mt. Zion, Mt. Moriah, the Mountain of Olives, AND HE SHALL COME BACK ATOP THE MOUNTAIN ON JUDGMENT DAY! "… for he cometh, for he cometh to judge the earth:he shall judge the world with righteousness, and the people with his truth."[Psalm96:13]. Yes, we die with Jesus to live FOREVER! Hence, mortal death is one poem all of us should learn to remember with every sunrise and sunset that come and go, even when the pot of gold is just a hand's reach away…

EPISTASIS. A SONG OF LIFE, AN ODE TO ETERNITY:A WIDOW'S EPISTOLARY. Dear Human,…when was the first time you laughed like the bubbling fountains, brooks, and springs of Mt. Gilboa? Do you still remember how genuine joy and happiness made your heart leap it almost bounced to heaven? Of course, your heart knows how that moment felt! When was the first time you heard of the time machine? Did you ever wish you could pass forward to some century where machines are perfectly brilliant almost totally human except that they don't have a sinful heart and a restless soul? Or, did you rather wish to go back in time to correct every awful mistake, all the terrible wrongs you have done, and dance the boogie with your pets and loved ones to sunrise? Where were you when the first dew kissed the bashful blossom? Were you able to paint how the roses blushed, how the tulips swayed, how the lichens beamed in the sunlight? Which lake, which river, which sea did you find yourself in a dreamful canoe? Why were the clouds so nice they gave you all the time to write your wishes upon the stars that even the moon fell in love with your secret wiles? Oh, those days, months, and years of adventure filled your basket with the awesome dream buds of nature and your bucket with the outpouring of hope and oh, the courage of faith! But today, why are you as blinded as the heart of Othello? How come you desire but streaks of blood upon the sun that magnanimously gives you all the warmth, the fun, and the best times of your life? Why do you see the terrors of Macbeth in the mirror? What demons have you allowed to thrive in your heart? How come you desire to exist like the cursed witches in the meandrous vastness of nothingness? Why do you now wish to smother yourself upon that world that accompanied you to your dreams and listened eagerly to your prayers? What has made you lose your songs, your poems, and your prayers? Is the silver lining too good to be true? Has it lost its magic in your sight? Is Pandora too powerful, turning your life upside down that Prometheus has to spring back to the duty of craftmanship? Are there so many trails you just can't make your choice? Or, have you given up to the dark that no epic, no legend shall ever again be echoed beyond the borders of time? What has become of you…what has become of you? The phoenix awaits the poet to write once more the verses…the nun prays for your soul, the priest is ready for your penance, the world is expectant of your light…are you not bothered the lamp is needy, waiting for the oil that should come from your toil? What now, human? Is the burden greater than your heart? Are your tears the poison of love? Can't the bracts, the epicalyxes hold your grief to the winds of rage? Is death too empty, meaningless, and vapid you just want to disappear before the bursting oasis of eternal happiness? Would you rather jump from that towering steel of pride, fear, and gloom or choose to take with courage and hope both the foreseeable and unforeseen blows, so you can pick up the pieces of your broken dreams and shattered life? Would the barren coldness of purgatory rest your soul, the endless fires of eternal damnation take away your sorrow? Is there no flash of the burning bush to make you believe once more the voice of God? Are your doubts too crippling you can't beat their challenge, that no candle could ever give its luminance, no star ever can diminish that angst no matter how luminiferous and bright the heavenly constellation? Or perhaps, there is that one moment to say, AMEN! This is my fourth book. But it's only the inspiring, luminous eloquent ordinariness of a man's faith that taught my words to be free of, and from too much burden! Jesus came in a manger. He had a carpenter for a father, and a simple village woman for a mother.

Nazareth was a plain village yet it was the cradle, the buiding ground for the Holy Work Of Salvation as the child, Jesus grew up in its soil, water, air, and skies. So ordinary but so perfectly beautiful! The great faith of Kulas resembles that of the other ordinary man, nailed on the cross beside Jesus who simply believed and accepted God in his heart despite of him dying, and in so much pain; Dimas, in all his remorse, humility, faith, and courage asked Jesus to remember him in Paradise! HE MADE HIS CHOICE! And he earned the reward of the DIGNITY OF HIS PAIN the moment he sought God's DIVINE MERCY AND LOVE! As ordinary but as profound, as beautiful as BETHLEHEM! Kulas, a poor farmer, is rich in the true joys of a simple life because he chooses to be happy, to unburden himself from the excessive weight of the world, hence, free in spirit; his faith much like of the good shepherds out there in the cold when the STAR shone SO BRIGHT! Whence their hearts received the Holy Ghost, their souls burned in the fire of the Miracle of the True Manger, emitting light in the dark, in thousands of years, for countless flocks of sheep, especially for the lost to be found and saved!

Now, I love with the birds. I breathe again, with the air...the winds of my childhood, of that great true love, of every lyric of our theme song, "The Wind Beneath My Wings." I'm taking my son, and our pets, oh with our newest family member, the pregnant PARISHIA JULY [who just came licking my purple shoes while JP and I were hearing mass at the Church of the Holy Sacrifice just recently! What a wonderful sign from God!] back to JERUSALEM! This time, I must lead to find THE TRAIL...with the Good Samaritan Woman who keeps appearing in so many ways whenever I and my son are in trouble [my late husband's colleague in UPD, Dr. Fe Nava who generously would give her precious time to me and my child, our dear *Ninang* Net Corpuz, who'd silently, consistently monitor our wellbeing, Enzo's "working hands" friend by the Parish of the Holy Sacrifice who keeps warmly smiling to us with her broken teeth everytime we go there for evening mass, Erlinda R. Aminov, the beautiful visitor in the notary public's office who smiled at me like she were my wild rare blue orchid, my late sister, *Manang* Erleen[!], that friendly helpful widow in Ilocos LTO, *Manang* Carolyn and Joy Custodio, from the land down under and the Mountain province respectively, who'd send spiritual food by private messaging or even a real book, and many more kind, helpful, and loving faces! Even be-spectacled Paulynn of Pan De Manila, Kalayaan whose persona and smile just warmed and cheered my heart as she handed me my hot Pan de Sal! Upon seeing her come out of their kitchen, I felt she just stepped out of a fun book of adventure or fairytale to fascinate my lowly pen once more! Yes, this woman of Jesus, this SAMARITAN WOMAN, she has always been there since I was but little excited feet and hands in open spaces, in riddles of trees and running waters! And with the "THREE KINGS," the Chosen Magi to protect, and who never fail to come with their genuine gifts of love and help [the good Indonesian SVD priest, the noble Igorot, the humble Bicolano], as well as very special prophets and kind-hearted shepherds like my second family in the UNITED STATES! Yes, our Guardians of Light are with us! They are indeed many to accompany us in our PILGRIMAGE back to the Holy Manger, our loved ones, our friends, total strangers, of course, our pets, my little pen, my readers, humanity, the world! The Man On The Cross sends so many to help me and my child to get back to our life of true bliss, of steadfast faith, a life with Jesus and the Holy Family! I must brace and prepare myself with more prayers and greater hope, to find THE TRAIL as I make the BRAVE CHOICE to take, to move forward to the Direction of LIGHT! I know in my heart it's going to be a long difficult journey, uncertain, full of danger, pitfalls, and temptations but THE GRACE OF MY PENITENCE shall bring all the help, THE BRIGHT STAR to guide in the threatening darkness until the HOLY MANGER is found and reached!

My husband wrote on the first page of the Holy Bible under the Acacia tree, by the stream, willows, and the farms of Bustos, Bulacan in 1992: "Dearest Emy, This is the literature of God…the best book in the whole world! This is also the" literature of our extra-ordinary and everlasting love! I will always love you! Blue Angel

We were then in A FARM. Enzo was A FARMER. He called himself, Blue Angel, our love everlasting. When I was a child, the noble *Igorot* put on my neck a garland of Everlasting, every day, I was copying the words in the Book of Life, and was it a blue mantle with the most beautiful of blue roses I touched? While the child's memory might have erred, the MIRACLE dwells in my heart! I have every reason to live again.

# A SONG FOR THE CHILD, A ROSE FOR JERUSALEM

you were a child of the open fields, friend of the soil
and everything of its good magical sprout and
fruit; trees were your sepulchres of
thought and knowledge; streams, brooks, fountains, and
springs taught you to be cheerful and laugh while the rain and the
sun showed the true face of life;
though Sleeping Beauty knew of your destiny
the Great Mountain just let you be, free as
the air so you can enjoy the rainbow when
it came and to seek the caves in times of
dread; nature was your home as you slept
and dreamt but then you were never
alone with your good allies of the Earth;
He was always with you as you played
each day with His Book; since that time,
He was already guiding your hands
not just for the dishes to wash but for
tales to write for the world in tearful seasons of your
life; and He sent you The Woman in
Blue Roses one high noon of your
adventure in the Glory of Light…to remind
you to always keep the Spirit, the Fire

in that heart; never to turn away,
never to lose hope, never to hate nor resist
the Cross; you were then in glee and
in mirth as you tumbled
and rolled on the ground that was
to become one dreary April day
the sepulture of your beloved...
indeed He was then preparing you
even when you were still but a child;
that fresh gust of wind on a lovely
summer noon, gave you what your
heart wished as you wore your little
apron, and life felt the Joy of Bethlehem!
your home was full, whole, and complete;

it radiated Love, it rejoiced in Grace,
it was Faithful even in the perilous dark;
the Family grew in prayer and in tears,
the tides came, the nights turned into
frightful nightmares, but the Fire to Live
withstood the coldest hours, the bleakest
of hope and dreams; A ROSE bore the
tempest to welcome the father, the mother,
and their child to The Trail...
they followed it with their animals,
guided by The Star, O Love that burned
like Tongues of Fire! the Gift of the Manger
gave seven years and seven zillions more!
indeed, the Miracle of Eternity comes in the
most unexpected of places, even if it's not
really deserved...that's how God works,
that's how beautiful Divine Love is!
The human heart just needs to keep beating,
however pained, however broken, however
burdened...Jerusalem is Real, not only in
December, not just in Israel, but

in Love, Hope, and Faith!
yes, my home was there, all three of us were
in that Manger…close, it was close, very
near the Holy One…we didn't know then,
but the JOY was real, we basked in it
as we lived our lives!
Today, my son and I shall go back…
The Trail is laid with blue roses, nothing to fear, nothing to fear! candles
are lighted, their wicks steady, ready for the winds, ready for the dark;
Our Mother of Perpetual Help is praying
for us as she is joined by Enzo,
her devoted son! yes, the journey back
waits for the widow and orphan but the
Good Flock is joining them! the Guardians of Light
are coming as widow and son once again peregrinate
to the Manger; Kitty now rests but
the Story of Jerusalem must be shared,
its Mystery to kindle more Fire, to give
more Light, to live one's life out of darkness,
out of the devil's lair, but
IN THE CONSUMING INEFFABLE RADIANT GLORY OF
GOD'S AMAZING GRACE, HIS DIVINE MERCY AND LOVE!
AMEN.
"OUR FEET SHALL STAND WITHIN THY
GATES, O JERUSALEM."[PSALM 22:2]

# SPIRITUAL CUPULE: *My Awakening*

I HAVE ALWAYS WONDERED WHY the religious and missionaries would ever be constantly present in my life...since I was a child and up to this day. Many of my childhood afternoons were spent with the different religions right there in the blissful *sala* of our home. The Catholic lay missionaries, the Protestants, the Iglesia Ni Kristo, the Baptists, the Mormons, the New Churches, even Islam would teach me at eight, nine years old so many things of a supernatural being, of Jesus, and Paradise. My morning playtime was mostly of WRITING. At eight years old, I was fascinated with the HOLY BIBLE, that I'd then be secretly copying it on my bond papers almost every day, when I could barely understand English, and my writing was still too crooked. My parents were devout Catholics, just like my granny, ALEJANDRA, and our Aunt MAURA who'd live in a huge wooden house with an equally fantastic garden nearby our modest bungalow. Both these beautiful "odd" women, aside from my elegant lovely Spanish-descent mother, who was a devotee of OUR LADY OF LOURDES, would intoxicate and surround me with overflowing FAITH with the way they lived, struggled, and prayed. *Auntie* Maura, until now at 92 is effervescent in her faith, mumbling the HOLY ROSARY, though she's now suffering with Alzheimer's. As I read more of the biblical inspired books our loving *PAPANG* ELOY would buy for us, six offspring then, my heart fattened in such amazing delight and joy with Abraham, David, Isaac, Joshua, Moses, Miriam, and MARY. I'd then develop an unusual proclivity or interest for church bells, belfries, and religious images, in wood, or simply pictures that I'd decorate my own bedroom later in life with these. In decades after, a very PRAYERFUL MAN, who called himself "BLUE ANGEL" with a BLUE JANSPORT KNAPSACK, full of religious "potpourri" would then sweep me off my feet, and become MY HUSBAND. He would take care of me not just as a beloved, his wife, but as a woman for God. ENZO would teach and inspire me how to be truly humble, patient, grateful, loving, and most of all, FORGIVING. He sensed I was to cheat on him during the latter part of our marriage. I was so LOST IN EREBUS because of my own fears. I was also very sick with PSYCHOSIS, possibly a result of the tragic death of my sister-soulmate which could have severely traumatized my brain. I was on medication. This smart young man came. He seduced me morning, noon, evening, and midnight. He was very attractive as he smiled like the Achillean Brad Pete of "TROY." But my husband LOVED ME TOO MUCH that he taught me HOW NOT TO SIN AND FALL IN THE TRAP OF TEMPTATION. He simply kept loving and taking good care of me. HE PRAYED MORE AND MORE WITH ME AND OUR LITTLE CHILD. I was SAVED from the PHANTOM OF FEAR AND ITS VERY TEMPTING INCUBUS! I was likewise grateful to my own brand of incoherent but liberating fiction and poetry. Back then in childhood, I was unusually observant, very auditory, very olfactory, very gustatory, overly TACTILE. Our *MAMANG* LOURDES loved the most marvellous and delicate of veils that she'd wear to church for different religious occasions, so were *LILANG* ANDANG, *AUNTIE* MAURA, and the pious WOMEN OF ILOCOS SUR. As a child, I was so drawn to these magically enthralling pieces of lace, that my little hands would just keep touching them until I'd be drowsy, and sleep in the wonderful worlds of secret, hidden worlds but which some beautiful LADY would always be SMILING AT ME. Until one day, when the sun was shining too bright, and my hands, my fingers were just too covered with soil as I was playing with earthworms, while building my perfect house or castle, and then rolling myself like an Indian war girl. She came for me, SMILING IN INCOMPARABLE RADIANCE, to touch her dazzling transluscent BLUE DRESS WITH BLUE ROSES. Maybe it was a DAYDREAM. I am not sure of that. But MY HEART kept it through the years. While I'd be teaching in so many schools, colleges, and universities, including Major Seminaries or Schools of Theology, in the Philippines, nuns, priests, novices, seminarians, missionaries, faithful believers would always be around sitting in my classes, or visiting me and my family at home, celebrating and rejoicing with us on happy occasions and the yuletide season, or simply, being loyal friends with me, helping me throughout the years, especially upon the death of my husband. My wedding choir was a strong twelve-man foreign JESUIT SEMINARIAN-"BLUE HERD" from TWELVE DIFFERENT COUNTRIES. Well, I thought because I waited twelve long years to be married to the man I so loved until eternity. Before I even stepped to high school, I was already very fond of religious pictures. As a young high school English teacher in my FIRST teaching assignment, ST. MARY'S COLLEGE, Quezon City, I was more than obsessed to read the lives of saints. Then the RELIGIOUS OF THE VIRGIN MARY[RVM] SISTERS would ask me to edit volumes of documents for the BEATIFICATION OF MOTHER IGNATIA DEL ESPIRITU SANTO. As I was with MARYKNOLL [MIRIAM] HIGH SCHOOL, I'd then compose a poem titled, "I OFFER YOU MY SONG" which would rekindle that childhood dream of becoming a "MONGHA, a sister-monk tending to roses while praying" as influenced by that FIRST NOVEL I read, "LILIES OF THE FIELDS." However, the namesake of the FIRST FILIPINO SAINT, ENZO RUIZ, became my professor and I fell in love with him as I was to inform my family I wanted to be a PINK SISTER. While I was with Ateneo de Manila University, I would then meet the GOOD JESUIT who would officiate my church wedding amidst the terrible pain our entire family was facing then, the terminal ailment [stage four brain cancer] of our beloved, my dearest dearest older sister, *MANANG* ERLEEN, whose four kids all went to the BLUE EAGLES University. The same Jesuit priest assisted me and our clan during the most difficult days and weeks as our beautiful sister gradually succumbed to the worst type of malignant brain tumor. FR. MANUEL "MANNY" FLORES, SJ would thereafter be most instrumental in leading me back to my "childhood fascination of secret BIBLE writing" but this time FOR THE WHOLE WORLD TO READ. In 2006, he sent to me a man who offered much of his later life to an APOSTOLATE IN THE UK, EUROPE, and the UNITED STATES OF AMERICA. This man was FRANK T. VILLA, who then asked me to help him write his BIOGRAPHY. He also studied at the "BLUE" university for his MBA. I was 41 years old, and just resigned from ATENEO, the blue eagles' nest.

Now, I am fifty-five. I do not know if my life is blessed for this mission, of WRITING FOR THE FATHER'S KINGDOM. I do not know if I am one of those favored "children." I do not know if my experience at eight years old was a surreal phenomenon or a supernatural encounter. I do not know why I am writing about it now. I do not know if that ethereal magazine picture of a blue rose held to her nose by a little girl also in total light blue countenance and backdrop affected my vision or fantasy. I do not know if my faith is a living faith. I do not know if my life is a lie. I do not know if this book is a curse. But what I am sure of is that I love JESUS CHRIST. "The lamb shall stand upon Mt. Zion…"[Revelation 14]

THERE'S NOTHING LIKE SPENDING CHRISTMAS
IN THE REAL SPIRIT OF JERUSALEM!
BUT TO LIVE EACH DAY IN ITS MIRACLE
IS TO CELEBRATE THE GRACE OF LIFE
TO THE FULLEST!
LET US LEARN TO FORGIVE EVERYONE AND
OURSELVES, NO MATTER HOW LONG IT
TAKES; PRAY, LOOK FOR THE TRAIL,
TO BASK IN THE GRACE OF PENITENCE! NO LOST
CHANCES, JUST A CHOICE TO MAKE!"…and thou shalt see
the good of JERUSALEM all the days of thy life."[Psalm 128:5b].

---THE END---

IN LOVING MEMORY OF MY LATE HUSBAND, Lorenzo Orillos
[AUGUST 10, 1947-APRIL 11, 2017]
I WILL ALWAYS LOVE YOU
"FOR BETTER OR WORST,
'TIL DEATH DO US PART"...NO GOOD-BYES,
JUST MEMOIRS OF THAT GREAT
WONDERFUL LOVE
OF EIGHT THOUSAND SEVEN HUNDRED SIXTY
AND A HUNDRED MORE SUNSETS...
ONE EVERLASTING LOVE, APRIL 1992-APRIL
2017, UP DILIMAN, PHILIPPINES
EMELY BATIN-ORILLOS [AUGUST 2019] THE
CAGE CLEANERS OF JERUSALEM

*Appendices*

Lightning Source UK Ltd.
Milton Keynes UK
UKHW040603181219
355568UK00004B/76/P